A Guide to Faithfulness Groups

Groups

Marcelle Martin

Inner Light Books
San Francisco, California
2019

A Guide to Faithfulness Groups

Grateful acknowledgment is made for permission to reprint from copyrighted material. To *Friends Journal* to reprint edited versions of the following pieces: "Called" by Marcelle Martin © 2011 Friends Publishing Corporation; "Finding a Quaker Charism at the Wild Goose Festival" by Viv Hawkins © 2013 Friends Publishing Corporation; "Questions of the Grail" by Viv Hawkins © 2016 Friends Publishing Corporation. To *What Canst Thou Say?* to reprint "Holy Accompaniment: the Gift of the Peer Group" by Ken Jacobsen et al. © 2017 *What Canst Thou Say?*

Editor: Charles Martin
Copy editor: Kathy McKay
Layout and design: Matt Kelsey

Published by Inner Light Books
San Francisco, California
www.innerlightbooks.com
editor@innerlightbooks.com

Library of Congress Control Number: 2019905051

ISBN 978-1-7328239-4-5 (hardcover)
ISBN 978-1-7328239-5-2 (paperback)
ISBN 978-1-7328239-6-9 (eBook)

Scripture quotations are from the New Revised Standard Version Bible, copyright © 1989 National Council of the Churches of Christ in the United States of America. Used by permission. All rights reserved worldwide.

Contents

Introduction

Throughout history, those who have been guided by divine Wisdom and then faithfully followed the leading of the Spirit have experienced divine love and healing power flowing through them into the wider world. God leads faithful individuals and groups to undertake particular actions and ways of life. Some are led to follow what has been variously named a call, leading, ministry, covenant, or spiritual commitment. Courageously faithful people have catalyzed important social changes and have been a force for reconciliation, education, peace, justice, and healing. Following the divine call is not easy, however, when it guides us to live and act in ways different from the prevailing culture. To be faithful, most people require the support of at least a few companions who understand how the Spirit leads individuals and groups to undertake specific actions and ministry and who also understand how to support one another in responding to those calls. In our time, the call to faithfulness is urgent, and people need practices that support both a deeper awareness of the movement of the Spirit and a courageous responsiveness.

Opportunities to speak openly about one's faith are becoming increasingly rare in our society. A recent *New York Times* article described poll results showing that, in most circles, people are speaking less often about spiritual topics. Out of 1,000 U.S. adults questioned, more than twenty percent had not had a spiritual conversation in the past year, and sixty percent said it was rare for them to do so. Only seven percent claimed to have had regular conversations about spiritual matters. This decrease in speaking freely about one's faith was reported even among members of faith communities. According to the article, computer analysis of published texts shows that usage of "most religious and spiritual words" has been declining steadily for more than a hundred years. Even language related to virtue and morality has declined; the use of "words such as 'love,' 'patience,' 'gentleness,' and 'faithfulness' has become much rarer. Humility words, such as 'modesty,' fell by fifty-two percent. Compassion words, such as 'kindness,' dropped by fifty-six percent. Gratitude words, such as 'thankfulness,' declined by forty-nine percent."[1]

When there is only limited public conversation about the spiritual life, and when the vocabulary used to describe it declines in use, it becomes harder to be a social person and maintain a lively, growing faith. In a world where there are strong pressures to conform to stifling cultural norms, faithfulness groups offer a simple, flexible, and durable practice that allows people to speak openly about their faith, reveal deep spiritual truths they may have concealed even from themselves, and mutually nurture Spirit-filled alternatives to contemporary ways of living.

For centuries, Quakers have developed spiritual practices and corporate structures that help people pay attention to the movement of the Spirit, discern divine guidance, and support one another in faithfully carrying out the tasks that God gives us. Although many of the practices described in this book were refined in Quaker community, they are suitable for any person, or community of faith, for anyone seeking to serve the love and wisdom that wants to work through human beings to create a better world, whether or not you call that larger reality God. This book explains what faithfulness is and how it can be cultivated by a community that practices ways to listen inwardly together for divine guidance.

Above all, this book is a guide to faithfulness groups, a practice that holds great potential for supporting individuals of any faith in allowing the work of the Spirit to become manifest through them and their communities. These groups are based on the understanding that each person has direct access to true spiritual guidance from within and that spiritually sensitive people can help one another tune in to that direct guidance. Faithfulness groups are composed of three to six people who meet on a regular basis to accompany each other on the journey of faithfulness over time. Most often, these groups meet in the homes of participants or at a meetinghouse or church. Leadership in the group is shared. Each person has about an hour of the group's focus every second or third meeting. Over time, faithfulness groups can develop a loving and deep spiritual intimacy that helps participants open more fully to the divine Presence within and sharpen their discernment of the subtle ways in which the Spirit communicates and leads. Participation in a faithfulness group can affect many aspects of the members' lives, helping people to be more alive in their faith and better able to participate fully in the spiritual life of their communities.

Introduction

Faithfulness groups can help people at any stage in listening for the promptings of the Spirit. Before writing this book, I sent a survey about faithfulness groups to several dozen Quakers who had participated in such groups, several for less than a year and others for much longer, including some who had participated for more than a decade. Of the fourteen who responded to the survey, a few gave brief answers to the survey questions, while others offered lengthy comments.

All who responded wrote of the benefits of such groups. One participant wrote that "my participation in my faithfulness group has stirred some leading within me, the glimmer of a way opening. I have been moved both by the inspiration of others in my group and because I have opened myself to larger possibilities of spiritual growth than I had previously imagined or permitted." Another, who had already been involved in an ongoing discernment process, has found that her faithfulness group "is a place where I can 'sound' the promptings I believe are coming from Spirit, learn to trust their validity, and open myself to allowing the way to open." Another participant wrote, "In articulating leadings, struggles, or opportunities, I have become much clearer about my experiences and gifts."

Those who have already clarified the nature of their call or leading to a particular course of action find a faithfulness group helpful in their discernment about how to make the changes that are necessary and how to take the active steps to which they are called. In addition to helping with discernment, the group provides ongoing loving companionship to those taking courageous risks. Faithfulness groups have supported leadings, calls, and ministries of all kinds, including parenting, caring for and accompanying others, building and nurturing community, teaching, creating art, traveling with a message, leadership, public witness, and social activism. One participant writes, "My faithfulness group supported my early leadings to create a play that included a traumatic experience in my life. Their continued support, love and accompaniment went a long way to making the creation of that play." Summing up her experience of being in a faithfulness group, she wrote, "It has deepened my spiritual life, it clarifies my path. The love of my faithfulness group helps me see that of God within me and my spiritual gifts."

Those who have been following a call or carrying a leading for a period of time find that participation in a faithfulness group helps not only with ongoing discernment of next steps but also with repeatedly renewing the faith and courage required to continue in the service, witness, or action to which they are called. Meeting with one's group provides regular opportunities to find spiritual refreshment and renewal while faithfully carrying on sometimes discouraging long-term efforts.

Widespread participation in faithfulness groups has the potential to bring greater spiritual vitality to the lives of individuals, meetings, congregations, and spiritual communities. Cultivating a culture of deep faithfulness brings forth the divine energy, wisdom, and guidance we need to adequately address the challenges of our time and learn to flourish on our planet in a new way.

This book contains guidelines for faithfulness groups and describes a range of practices that may be helpful in such groups. It tells the story of an imaginary faithfulness group session that uses several of these practices, and it names some of the fruits experienced by participants of such groups. Also included are quotations by people who have participated in faithfulness groups. In appendix A, you will find descriptions of several group processes that have a similar purpose to faithfulness groups. The appendices that follow contain writings by others about faithfulness groups and related group processes. In the back of this book is a list of written and online resources as well as a glossary of some of the Quaker terminology used in these pages.

Faith and a Culture of Faithfulness

All who are led by the Spirit of God are children of God.
—Romans 8:14 NRSV

Faith arises from an understanding or perception that reality is vaster than the physical world and that our lives are lovingly sustained by something larger than ourselves, which we call God. Over time, faithful people have found many ways to name their understanding of the Divine, including God, Creator, Almighty, Holy Spirit, and Christ. Today, many often speak simply of the Spirit or the Light. Faith may begin with beliefs, but it grows to become more about a lived relationship with God. Faith involves trust in the loving intent of the larger divine reality in which we live. Faith also calls us to participate in manifesting God's love and truth in every arena of life, including bringing peace and healing into situations of suffering, injustice, or conflict, and working for a sustainable future.

Faith grows as we become aware of divine reality and enter into a conscious relationship with it. Doing so requires a tender heart, an openness to subtle inner impressions and movements of the Spirit, and a willingness to notice how the divine presence shines in others and comes alive in events and interactions between people. As we pay attention in this way and notice more clearly the presence, activity, and love of God within us and in our lives, we want to make more space for the Holy. We become eager to open more fully to the gifts and blessings of the Spirit.

Almost everyone has moments when they sense something holy in themselves. Many have glimpses of how love shapes people and infuses the world in a sacred way. Yet, in a culture that largely denies spiritual reality and usually ignores spiritual awareness, we risk rejection when we speak of our direct experience of such things. Familial and cultural conditioning reinforces this, teaching

5

most of us to disregard the stirrings of our souls and ignore the still, quiet voice of God until we rarely, if ever, hear it. This is generally the case even if we grow up with a strong concept of God and a belief in spiritual reality. When our faith is focused primarily on what we believe rather than on what we directly perceive and experience, our attention is trapped in our thinking processes. Limiting thoughts and fears narrow our perception of reality.

For our relationship with God to grow, we must surrender our tight personal control and become willing to follow where the Spirit leads. We learn to attend better to our own souls and also to relate to other people in undefended ways. As the promptings of the Spirit become clearer to us and we become more responsive, we learn to trust the Spirit to guide us. Often, at first, this guidance relates to our personal lives, work, and relationships. Gradually, however, we are also led to participate in some way in making visible the reality of heaven on earth.

Quakers use three related words to describe the process of being led by God into action. The first is *concern*. As people grow in the life of the Spirit, they become increasingly sensitive to everything that is false, unjust, or contrary to love and harmony. The suffering caused by deception, injustice, injury, or oppression becomes more evident and more painful.

Rather than feel the burden of *all* suffering and injustice, an individual or community usually becomes especially sensitive to the harm being done in particular situations. They begin to experience the weight or burden of a specific concern. The concern may relate to unhealthy or unholy dynamics in the small circle of a family or community, or in the larger circles of society and the world. Those upon whom a concern is placed are drawn to learn more about the situation and those affected by it. Sometimes people speak of feeling "exercised" about a particular situation, troubled by the Spirit to deeply contemplate the causes and effects.

Eventually, a person or group carrying a concern is prompted by the Spirit to undertake specific actions to address the issue. A God-given task is referred to as a *leading*. Outward events may be closely connected to the emergence of a leading, but a leading always also has the sense of being spiritually prompted from within. A leading might relate to a particular action of short or long duration. The word *call* is used to describe a God-given task that demands effort and attention over a long period of time, and

6

it may involve several leadings. A person may first feel the call before any leadings are experienced, sometimes starting in childhood.

Leadings and calls are not general principles that can be learned from reading the Bible or devotional books. Genuine leadings from God are in harmony with the teaching of Scripture but they are also very specific promptings guided by God or the Spirit from within. These promptings may be to be of service to one's family or community through acts small and large; the service may be short term or extend over decades. As in biblical times, people today may also be led by God to prophetic acts and the exercise of spiritual gifts, including offering divinely inspired messages, teaching, preaching, nurturing the faith of others, living in certain ways, modeling alternatives to the current culture, serving those in need, giving witness, and taking radical nonviolent action to counter dangers or evils in society.

It can be difficult to know for sure when a prompting to action comes from God or from another source. People are motivated by a multitude of impulses and beliefs, many of them unconscious and some deeply embedded in culture and upbringing. It is important, therefore, to test leadings with others. If a leading comes from God and not from a purely personal motivation, cultural conditioning, or social pressure, others who are attuned to the Spirit can also sense its source. An important question in discerning a leading is to ask if it leads to the fruits of the Spirit named in Galatians 5:22: love, joy, peace, patience, kindness, goodness, faith, gentleness, and self-control. Other important questions to ask are, "Does the leading fulfill God's purposes rather than the desires of the ego?" "Does the leading persist even when a person or group is faced with obstacles or the resistance of others?" Testing a leading may involve taking a step, observing what happens both inwardly and outwardly, and noting what is learned.

Often, important information related to a leading and its source comes when one or more initial steps are taken. Sometimes taking those initial steps may be all that God is actually calling for, and then the sense of having a leading may be withdrawn. In other cases, following a leading to completion may turn out to be a first step toward a larger call and greater commitment.

Someone who has felt a concern and then followed a leading to take a particular kind of action usually grows in awareness about the issue of concern and those affected by it. A new leading may emerge next, followed later by other steps. While some people may hear God calling them long before receiving a particular leading, others may follow one or more leadings before they recognize them as part of a larger call on their life.

In learning to discern the movements of the Spirit in oneself and in one's life, it becomes necessary to find companions who are aware not only of the divine reality but who also appreciate the complexity of human motivation. The Spirit's invitation to sensitive openness is in conflict with the social forces that teach people to be wary and defensive. Usually without being explicit about it, our culture trains people from birth to shut off their perception of spiritual reality. Even people who are religious, therefore, often find it difficult or rare to sense God's presence. Faith that is based only on ideas, doctrines, or beliefs is thin and brittle, and such a faith sometimes focuses on things that are not truly of God. Stories of Jesus, the prophets, and people of faith can point us toward divine reality and teach us about God's ways, but growing in true faith requires more than stories, doctrine, or the outward forms of religion. It requires encountering the divine presence active in our lives; it requires direct knowledge and experience of the Spirit. Whatever our beliefs, it generally takes time to open our hearts to the work of the Spirit within and through us.

We have a divided nature. At birth, we come into the world blazing with the divine Light and overflowing with love, sensitive to the spiritual realm from which our being has emerged. We are deeply connected to our souls, which have a purpose in the divine cosmic plan. Yet, the wonderful bodies into which we are born are strongly oriented to physical sensation and bodily survival. Our brains and nervous systems are hardwired to be alert for danger. Survival requires cooperation with others, and we crave acceptance and approval from family, friends, and society. Fear of losing our belonging keeps most people oriented to the physical world and eager for a secure place within their culture. The physical sensations and human interactions that capture our attention can overwhelm the subtle spiritual senses that testify to our interconnection with all things in the Spirit. Fortunately, with support from our faith community and/or from a close circle of

8

spiritual friends, we can learn to distinguish between the false conditioning we have absorbed and the promptings of the Spirit.

Often a person hearing a call or following a leading seeks the support of someone with deep experience of the spiritual life. This companion may be called a spiritual nurturer, spiritual friend, spiritual director, or perhaps an elder (whatever their age). Or, he or she may not have any of these labels but may simply seem wise and open to hearing how the Spirit is at work in others. Speaking and discerning one's call or leading with such a companion can be an important step in testing a leading. This kind of support may be needed in an ongoing way. Since Quakerism began, it has been common for those who travel to carry out a leading to take with them a companion, often an elder but sometimes simply another person also seeking to be faithful and to grow in the Spirit.

In addition to finding the one-on-one support of an elder or spiritual companion, Quakers today often use the process called the clearness committee to help each other discern leadings clearly. The focus of a two-hour (or longer) clearness committee meeting is on discerning a particular call or leading, usually felt by one person but sometimes by a pair or a group. A clearness committee typically meets only once, or at most two or three times, until clarity has been reached about what the Spirit is prompting the person or group to do.

After a call or leading has been discerned, a Quaker meeting may be led to appoint a committee to accompany the individual or group over time and provide oversight. Some meetings have so many members requiring support and oversight that a group is appointed to simultaneously accompany several people with calls and leadings. They all meet together on a regular basis. A committee appointed by a meeting to exercise care and oversight for those with leadings or particular forms of ministry is responsible for finding ways to inform the community about what is happening and to help keep the individual(s) connected with the life of the meeting, spiritual community, or congregation, especially when calls or leadings require people to travel away for periods of time. When faithfulness results in particular kinds of sacrifice or suffering, the committee with oversight may report this and ask the community for whatever help the faithful person or people require. Sometimes this includes financial support.

9

Whether or not one has identified a call or leading, people may find it helpful to participate in a faithfulness group, a small group that provides ongoing mutual spiritual accountability and support. Sometimes several people whose leadings have been recognized by their spiritual community form a faithfulness group together, perhaps gathering people from more than one meeting or church. It is not necessary, however, to have discerned a call or leading or to have received any kind of recognition from one's faith community in order to join a faithfulness group.

A faithfulness group serves multiple functions. It helps people pay attention to the truth of their soul, the guidance of their inner teacher or guide, and the promptings of the Spirit or God. In this way it provides an ongoing source of spiritual support. More than that, it also helps with discernment and clearness about calls and leadings, step by step. Once the promptings of the Spirit have been discerned, a faithfulness group lovingly helps its members to recognize for themselves and then clear away any impediments to faithfulness. It provides spiritual support to live the life to which the Spirit invites each person.

Quakers have a long history of using sacred listening circles of many sorts to help people become aware of God's presence, activity, and guidance. In addition to clearness committees and the committees that provide oversight and guidance for those with identified calls, leadings, and ministries, Quakers also use what we call "worship sharing groups" This more informal kind of circle provides an opportunity for a group to listen inwardly together to the truth in their hearts and to share the wisdom that is given to each. Often such circles gather only once to focus in a particular way. Some Quaker communities organize regular opportunities to participate in such circles. (More about various forms of sacred listening circles can be found in appendix A.)

The format for faithfulness groups is more recent. It emerged in 2005 out of a peer group process used by some participants in the Shalem Institute's program on spiritual guidance,[2] a program designed for people who serve as companions to those exploring their spiritual lives. The original teachers in that Shalem program, Gerald May, Tilden Edwards, and Rose Mary Dougherty, emphasized the importance of having peer support while offering spiritual companionship (or spiritual direction) to others. To be faithful to that particular ministry, they said, it was very useful to meet with other spiritual directors to reveal the blessings and inward challenges, resistances, and blocks that were coming up in the process of that service.

For nine years, I participated in a group of Quaker spiritual nurturers and spiritual directors; we met monthly to provide peer support to each other. We helped each other be faithful in the practice of nurturing the spiritual lives of others. Over the course of the years, our time together also helped each of us develop our discernment skills and hone our ability to help others explore their spiritual experiences.

In 2005, fellow Quaker Laura Melly and I were participating in that peer group while experiencing calls that included but were broader than the particular ministry of spiritual direction. At that time, we realized that this format could be opened up to offer peer support for any form of faithfulness—following a leading, living out a call, engaging in service, undertaking some sort of ministry, or being faithful in carrying out one's job or family commitments. With permission from Shalem Institute, we revised the peer group guidelines for wider use. Then we called together a group of Quakers who were seeking to be faithful to various kinds of calls and leadings. The first such group, formed in 2005, continues to meet fourteen years later, though many of the original members have moved away and others have joined. Initially, the group was called a peer group. As new groups formed, some took different names, including "spiritual accountability groups." In 2017 we adopted the name "faithfulness groups" to describe our intention and practice.

For many seeking to hear God's guidance and respond faithfully, participation in an ongoing faithfulness group has been a great blessing. Participants have supported each other in faithfully carrying out the work of their faith communities, engaging in environmental and political activism, traveling to speak or to lead workshops or retreats, serving as chaplains, working against racism, doing prison ministry, being a parent, creating theater performances, leading groups, and much more.

Participating in faithfulness (or peer) groups was an essential element of several long-term programs, including the Way of Ministry program in 2007–2008[3]; a second-year Spiritual Formation Program; and a six-month Called to Action program, all in the Philadelphia area. Quakers in New England have also offered programs in which such groups have been a key component, including a three-month blended learning course (in-person and online) in 2009–2010 entitled Practicing Spiritual Accountability. The faithfulness group process has also been taught in workshops at Pendle Hill Retreat Center, at several Friends General Conference Summer Gatherings, and elsewhere.

More recently, the 2017–2018 Nurturing Worship, Faith and Faithfulness Program, held at Woolman Hill Retreat Center, required all participants to form local faithfulness groups. Each of these groups included members of one or more Quaker meetings and sometimes people from outside the Quaker community. Participants found that these groups enlivened the spiritual life of the whole meeting. Some communities experienced so much interest in participation that two or three groups were formed.

Most people who participate in faithfulness groups have, at least to some extent, a sense of their soul or of a larger spiritual reality. They may feel this awareness mostly as a longing for a greater sense of purpose or meaning or a desire to live in a society based on love, truth, and justice. Many have had glimpses of the sacred nature of life and feel a desire to live with greater integrity. Some people's lives have been reoriented by spiritual experiences. Receiving the spiritual support of others, through participation in a faithfulness group and in other ways, becomes especially urgent after receiving a call or leading from the Spirit to take up a particular task or share certain truths more widely. It is challenging to maintain an orientation toward God, and it is helpful to be with others who want lives of meaning and true purpose that are oriented toward the divine Reality at the heart of everything. Meeting regularly with a faithfulness group can be a crucial aid in the process of centering our lives on God and becoming whole and undivided. Hearing about the efforts of others to sense God's leadings and respond faithfully helps each person in the group to better recognize inward spiritual guidance, trust providence, and welcome spiritual power when it wants to flow through us for the sake of others.

For many, participation in an ongoing faithfulness group is a form of sacred companionship that nurtures growth in the spiritual life. It is not necessary to have a clear sense of a concern, leading, or call in order to join a group. At first, and all along, a person's participation in the group may focus on getting to know who they are called to be as a person, what their soul wants, and how that fits or does not fit with the life they are currently leading. As one becomes better acquainted with the divine Mystery that gives us life, hearts open. Love and trust become more available. People experience a growing desire to put God or Spirit at the center of their lives and a growing need to be faithful to the promptings of the divine Love they discover alive within them. The call to participate in God's love for others becomes stronger.

Once clarity comes about how God is leading or calling us, it is time for courageous action, time to translate faith into faithfulness. Participants gain increasing access to the spiritual strength they need to act by absorbing the power and presence of God, which can often be felt in faithfulness group meetings. Being a witness to others who are seeking to be faithful encourages each group member to grow in the humble boldness that is often required for faithful action.

Guidelines for Faithfulness Groups

The purpose of faithfulness group meetings is to help participants pay attention to God's presence and activity as they seek to faithfully follow divine guidance in service, witness, following a leading, carrying out a ministry, or the activities of daily life. Faithfulness groups provide ongoing support, assistance with discernment, and spiritual accountability for group members. During a typical two-hour session, two people will be the focus of the group for about one hour each. Each focus person presents something about their current faith life and recent efforts, struggles, opportunities, or leadings to be faithful.

The role of the group is to prayerfully listen to the presentation and then, as prompted by the Spirit, to ask questions that may help the presenter explore more deeply their relationship to, awareness of, and response to the Spirit in their efforts to be faithful. Occasionally, group members mirror for the participant what they have witnessed. This process is a form of spiritual nurturing for the presenter as well as an ongoing committee for mutual clearness and accountability. Ideally, the group meets on an ongoing basis and leadership is shared by all. In the rotation, each member has a regular opportunity to be the focus of the group's attention.

Group Atmosphere: Holy Accompaniment

The faithfulness group is a practice of holy accompaniment. Group meetings are conducted with a prayerful, reverent, contemplative attitude. Participants listen in a relaxed yet very attentive way to one another and at the same time also notice their own inner responses, looking for the presence of the Spirit. The group is attentive to God in what is happening moment by moment, with the intention of helping one another be likewise attentive to the

Divine in daily life. Group members refrain from posing questions too quickly or in a forced manner. Instead, each person waits to sense and respond to the Spirit's movement, allowing questions to surface gently. Ample time for silence during the discussion is needed.

When the prayerful and contemplative atmosphere of the group slides into problem-solving, advice-giving, analysis, criticism, storytelling, or tangential discussions, it is important to recall the group's intention to listen for God and to return attention to the Spirit. Group members are responsible to attend to their own awareness in this way as well as to keep noticing the overall atmosphere of the group to see if some gentle correction might be needed, such as, "Could we have some silence right now?" or "I wonder if we can return to our focus?" The goal for each member is to gently try to hear and respond to the movement of the Spirit within the meeting of the group itself.

Focus of the Meetings

Each meeting should be carefully centered around experiences and concerns related specifically to the presenter's effort to be faithful. This includes how the faith and prayer experience of the presenter affects their faithfulness. In an attitude of open, humble, and holy accompaniment, the group maintains a focus on the presenter's spiritual concerns, experiences, feelings, faith, blocks, blind spots, gifts, discernment, confidence, and confusion in their effort to be faithful and in their reflection afterward.

It may be helpful for the presenter to ask the group for help paying attention to specific spiritual concerns, yet the presenter must avoid seeking advice or suggestions. The focus should not be upon other people or their experiences unless information about them might shed light on the presenter's condition, discernment, and faithfulness. Although it is often tempting to engage in problem-solving, this should be avoided. Keep the focus on the spiritual awareness of the presenter and on everyone's moment-by-moment attentiveness to the Divine. Doing so strengthens the presenter's ability to access spiritual guidance from within.

Presentations

Each presenter has fifteen minutes to tell the group about events, inner movements, and concerns related to their efforts to be faithful. The presentation may include a specific incident or interaction, or it may be a description of a particular faithful activity, service, leading, witness, or ministry as it has developed over time. It could be a follow-up on a situation that has been previously presented. It is up to the presenter to discern what material to present and what form this should take. This calls for prayerful reflection ahead of time. The presenter should always include some information about what they experience when they pray (or 'hold in the Light') the events and experiences, questions and concerns that they are bringing to the group. Presentations should include only enough information about others as is needed to provide an adequate understanding of the presenter's experience. Aspects of the presenter's service or ministry may require anonymity. If this is the case, the presenter may need to create a fictional name and disguise some identifying details about those they are serving.

Brief, Factual Questions of Clarification

After a presentation, the convener asks if there are any necessary, brief, factual questions of clarification. Group members only ask this sort of question if the presentation was not clear on an essential point and some quick clarification is required in order to understand the situation. The time needed for this clarification reduces the time available for deeper questions and exploration, so it is important to avoid asking questions that are motivated only by curiosity. It is not necessary for group members to fully understand a situation in order to be helpful to the presenter. Group members should only ask clarification questions that will help the group serve the presenter.

Questions and Deeper Exploration

After any brief questions of clarification, the group settles into a short period of silent prayer and worship, out of which deeper questions for the focus person are posed. Prompted by the Spirit, these questions are intended to help the presenter focus on what is happening in their relationship with God in their efforts to be faithful. Avoid asking questions just for the sake of asking questions. No straining or striving to come up with a question is needed. Silent, prayerful accompaniment provides an opportunity to sense questions that are being prompted by the Spirit and reduces the human tendency to fill silences that may feel empty but are not.

Faithfulness is aided by helping to make conscious any blocks within the presenter in order that they may seek divine assistance in dissolving them and become more clearly and immediately present to the reality of the Spirit in their efforts or struggles to be faithful. The faithfulness group format assumes that if the members of the group are openly and willingly attuned to the Spirit, any necessary assistance, learning, critique, and prayer will be expressed or revealed inwardly to the presenter, with the help of the group's prayerful presence and Spirit-led questions. Though it can be tempting to apply psychological interpretations to the presenter's behavior, challenges, and opportunities, this is not the work of the faithfulness group. Members are encouraged to maintain a humble, reverent attitude toward the work of the Spirit within the presenter.

Confidentiality

It is important to remember that everything shared in the group is confidential. Participants can speak about their own experience and learning in the group, but the stories and information shared by others should not be repeated. After the group meeting is over, it is also important that group members not initiate discussion with the presenter about confidential details or considerations related to their presentation. It is up to the presenter to initiate any further conversation about something that was presented.

Growing into the Format Together

In the beginning, as group members learn the discipline of this format, the faithfulness group practice can feel awkward. Open-hearted sharing and disclosure of one's spiritual challenges is a tender and occasionally uncomfortable experience, but as intimacy and trust develop, this becomes easier. Over time, groups learn how to accompany each other into deep realms of faithfulness.

Members become like experienced ensemble musicians, taking turns asking questions as they accompany one another with the guidance of the Holy Spirit that is working through the group as a whole.

The Schedule of a Faithfulness Group Meeting

The suggested schedule for each two-hour meeting is as follows:

1. OPENING—Convener briefly reminds group about the intended focus and attitude

2. PRAYER AND SILENT WORSHIP—5 minutes, led by convener

3. FIRST PRESENTATION—Up to 15 minutes; group listens silently to the presentation, and the presenter includes mention of his or her prayer about the situation

4. BRIEF, FACTUAL QUESTIONS OF CLARIFICATION (if necessary)

5. SILENT PRAYER AND REFLECTION—2 minutes

6. DEEPER QUESTIONS AND EXPLORATION—35 minutes total for 4, 5, and 6

7. BREAK—5 minutes

8. SECOND PRESENTATION—Up to 15 minutes

9. BRIEF, FACTUAL QUESTIONS OF CLARIFICATION (if necessary)

10. SILENT PRAYER AND REFLECTION—2 minutes

11. DEEPER QUESTIONS AND EXPLORATION—35 minutes total for 9, 10, and 11

12. EVALUATION OF THE MEETING—5 minutes; see guidelines in the next section

13. CLOSING WORSHIP—2 to 5 minutes

14. CLOSING

If the group meets for longer than two hours, additional time can be devoted to silence and prayer at the beginning, after the break, and at the closing. In addition, the break can be longer than five minutes.

Some groups meet for a meal together beforehand and use that time to hear from members who will not be presenting that day. Groups who do not share food first may want to meet for two and a half hours in order to allow for a brief "check-in" at the beginning from the members of the group who will not be presenters at that meeting.

If some group members have busy schedules and limited time, it is best to ensure that meetings stay within the two-hour schedule listed above.

Evaluating and Processing the Meeting

Before closing the meeting, the convener asks the group to reflect on the meeting, including the sense of prayerful presence within the group, noting what facilitated it and what seemed to get in the way. From the standpoint of the presenter and other group members, was there a sense of spiritual discernment happening for the presenter? Questions such as the following might help. In the five minutes allotted to this time of evaluation at the end of a meeting, it is rarely possible to discuss all of these questions. Over time, however, a group can reflect on each of the following:

1. How well did we stay focused on those who were presenting and their relationship with God rather than on the situation or those being served?

2. Were there any moments when we strayed from our focus? For example, did we engage in problem-solving or analysis or did group members tell their own stories?

3. What was the quality of our attention to the Spirit, and was there sufficient silence?

4. Did we all remain faithful to the inner Guide?

5. How was God able to work through us as a team?

Presenters might share which questions seemed to be especially helpful or describe a moment when they had a particular sense of the Spirit, experienced an inner ring of truth, or received a new insight. Or they might suggest what might have been more helpful, such as leaving more silence after each answer or at a specific point.

Over time, it may be helpful for the group to notice if patterns arise among them that make it difficult to stay focused on the presenter and that person's relationship with God. Do group members tend, for example, to ask questions too quickly, not leaving enough silence for presenters to absorb the truth of what they have just said? Does the group or certain members get hooked on a regular basis into offering suggestions or trying to solve problems? Does the group veer into psychological analysis?

The Presenter

Prayerful preparation helps presenters be more available to the gifts of the Spirit. The presentation can focus on any area of life in which the presenter is seeking to be faithful or wants to sense divine guidance about how to be or how to act. Some participants may wish to focus their presentations, over time, on a particular call from God or leading of the Spirit they are following.

In either case, in the days and weeks before your turn as a presenter, it is helpful to take some quiet moments to pray about the focus of the upcoming presentation. Inner guidance may come in the form of words, images, memories of specific moments, an awareness of a difficult issue, or a sense of something unclear or painful that needs attention. It may be helpful to jot down notes about what is experienced during these times of prayer.

A good presentation often includes an account of both inner experience and outer events. For some, it is tempting to give detailed background information. When presenting about a particular focus for the first time, take care to determine how much background information the other group members really need. It is not necessary to repeat what was shared in a previous presentation. Leave a good portion of the presentation time to speak about what has been happening very recently.

It is wise to pray and reflect in advance about the focus and specifics of a presentation, but when the moment comes to speak, allow yourself to be open to the immediate prompting of the Spirit. Looking at your notes may be helpful, or you may find that something fresh is being given for you to say in the moment. A group may find that it is sometimes helpful for the presenter to provide something in writing in advance of the meeting. If your group and you decide that this could be helpful, it is important for you, as the presenter, not to merely read your written statement but to give a spontaneous presentation during the group meeting. In the prayerful atmosphere of the group, what comes from the heart may be fresh and somewhat different from what was considered in advance.

This is your time. Pay attention to the divine Presence with you as you speak. Stop and wait in silence when you are not sure what to say next. There is no hurry. Allow the silent, prayerful attention of the group help you sense more clearly what is true.

If you attend to what is happening in your heart and allow yourself to speak in an open and vulnerable way, the sense of the presence of the Spirit may become stronger for you and for others. Trust God and the group to hold your story in a loving way. Allow yourself to say things that you may never have said aloud before. Listen to what you say and how it feels to say it.

During the time of questions, do not rush to respond. Look into your heart. Pause and wait when necessary. Sometimes the answers will come in a way that might surprise you—as an image, a Scripture passage, a line of poetry, a metaphor, a memory, a gesture, or a movement. Sometimes it is enough to sit with a question in silence for a moment. If no answer arises that is to be shared with the group, you can say so. Sometimes more understanding comes after the meeting is over. Sometimes living with a question is more important than receiving a particular answer.

If you feel some immediate guidance of the Spirit during the time of deeper questions, close your eyes and attend to what the Spirit is doing or saying within you. Allow the group to hold you in the Light as you commune silently with God. When it feels right, share what is happening.

Relax. There is no one right way to be during the time when the group focuses on you. You may feel that an answer you have just given is not quite accurate. This is good to notice, not a cause for reproach. The purpose of the group is to provide holy accompaniment as you and God, together, look at what the Spirit is doing as you attempt to be faithful. This time of focus in your group is an opportunity to grow in intimacy with the Spirit and to gain clarity about the nudges, calls, and leadings you may have experienced.

Even if there is no specific sense of clarity by the end of your focus time, you can inwardly give thanks for the attention that has been given and your growing awareness.

Reflecting on a Presentation

The focus of the faithfulness group is to help its members grow in faith and faithfulness in daily life, in service or witness, and/or in following a call or leading. The group's primary responsibility is to be present to each focus person in a loving, contemplative, nonjudgmental way that helps members open as fully as possible to the truth in their heart and to the activity and presence of God. The sets of questions below may help groups become sensitive to a wide range of issues that affect a person's ability to serve faithfully. These questions are useful for reflection before and after the group meets; they help group members consider many areas that may lead to fruitful exploration during the time of deeper questions. During the meeting, however, put the list of questions aside. Do not attempt to seek answers in an analytical way. These are questions for reflection before or after a session. While the group is listening to a presentation or helping a presenter enter into deeper exploration, a different kind of question—"evoking questions"—are what is needed. Evoking questions are discussed in the chapter Practices for Faithfulness Groups (see page 32).

The Role of Faith, Spiritual Openness, and Prayer

What theological language does the presenter use to speak of their spiritual experience and relationship with God? What spiritual beliefs inform or limit the way they perceive the events of their lives and the choices they make? How does their faith support them?

What is the presenter's degree of trust in God or the Spirit, and how much are they relying upon their own personal competence and willful effort? Is the presenter surrendering to the leadings of the Spirit or resisting? Are they surrendering to God, to their own fears and desires, or to the expectations of others?

How does the presenter pray about their call to faithfulness or about particular situations or contexts for their service, witness, leading, or ministry? How do they pray about others who are involved? What are the presenter's experiences and assumptions about what prayer is, how it happens, and the power it has?

What is the nature of the presenter's love and compassion in relationship with others and especially with those they may be called to serve? Is it personal? Does it feel spiritual? How deeply can the presenter touch the hearts of other people, seeing through surface images and emotions to the Light or to God's image in others?

Discernment

Is the presenter hearing or following a new call or leading, or have they been following a call for a while? How does this affect the presenter's sense of themselves, of God's presence, and of those served?

What is the nature of the presenter's awareness of or attention to God while attempting to be faithful? Can they look deeply into situations, events, and experiences to sense the work of the Spirit? What helps or hinders the presenter's spiritual attentiveness?

How does the presenter seek and discern the subtle guidance or movement of the Spirit within or through them? How do they test with others the promptings and leadings they experience?

Is the presenter seeking to be attentive to the workings of grace in the lives of others or in the actions they feel called to carry out?

Resistance

Has the presenter followed up on the spiritual guidance, nudges, and leadings they have received? If not, what is standing in the way?

How easily does the presenter look within themselves to discover their own fears and resistance to the leadings of the Spirit? Do they open these areas to the Light for healing and transformation? How does the presenter seek divine help in addressing inner impediments to faithfulness?

In what way does the presenter turn to God when faced with resistance from other people, institutions, and social structures? Do they trust God to guide them in facing both inner and outer resistance?

Accountability

Is the presenter staying true to spiritual priorities and commitments?

Is the presenter willing to wait for a clear leading or spiritual prompting before acting? Is it possible they are taking actions that have not yet been prompted by the Spirit, or are they lagging behind the Guide?

Is the presenter willing to speak truth in difficult situations when asked to do so? How well can the presenter address or confront challenging issues?

What help does the presenter require in order to respond faithfully to their leadings? Are they asking for the help they need? Are they taking action to enlist that help?

The Convener

It is the responsibility of the convener to open and close each meeting, to lead the worship and prayer time at the beginning of the meeting, to keep time carefully according to the schedule, to moderate the discussion as needed, and to attend to whether the discussion keeps to the intent, atmosphere, and attitude described in these guidelines. (The latter is the responsibility of all, but it is helpful if the convener is consciously attentive to this.) It is recommended that the convener remind the group at the beginning that the focus should be more on the presenter than on others who might be involved and that the basic intent of the meeting is to be open and responsive to the Spirit. This reminder can be in the form of reading a paragraph or two from these guidelines at the beginning of the group meeting.

After both presentations are finished and just before closing the group's time together, the convener asks everyone to reflect on how the meeting has been conducted. The convener may pose one question at a time or read all of them at once, giving time for group members to reflect and respond. Make sure that both of the focus people have a chance to comment on their experience of the process. After the group reflects on the particular sessions that have just taken place, the convener may be moved to invite the group to reflect on their experience over time. Have patterns become apparent that need to be addressed? Usually, not all questions can be covered in any particular five-minute evaluation session, but over time the group can consider all of the evaluation questions.

Conveners and presenters should be scheduled on a rotating basis, with one convener and two presenters for each two-hour meeting. A person should not serve as both convener and presenter during a given meeting.

The group may decide that it is the responsibility of the convener of the next meeting to send reminders to the group members about their upcoming meeting and about who will be presenting and convening.

Forming a Faithfulness Group

There are several ways to draw together a faithfulness group. One way is to consider the people with whom you would like to be in such a group and invite them. Another method is to make a general announcement in your faith community about faithfulness groups and invite anyone who is interested to explore the possibility. It is also possible to invite people from outside your faith community.

Above all, it is good to include people who have a longing for greater depth in their spiritual life and a desire for spiritual companionship in exploring how the Spirit is at work within them and in their lives. In considering possible group members, it is important to invite people who have the ability to patiently listen to others and to exercise discipline in their speaking.

Some groups are composed entirely of people who share a common call or ministry, such as groups whose members all engage in religious education, facilitate Alternatives to Violence Project workshops, or participate in environmental witness. Some groups are composed entirely of people from one faith community who share a common theology. Shared understanding and a common cause among participants can facilitate deep explorations. It can also be valuable, however, to be in a group whose members are called to different kinds of faithful service, study, or witness or to be in a group with people from different denominations or faith traditions. If everyone is willing to respect the faith of the others and be sensitive to the variety of ways that God can be thought about and experienced, the differences can lead to quite fruitful new perspectives and heart-opening experiences.

One faithfulness group participant found that participating in a group in which everybody was white and middle class was a frustrating experience for her. She felt she was constantly inviting the group into deeper intimacy, challenge, and interdependence than others were willing to engage in. She has subsequently had a richer experience in a group whose members come from more diverse backgrounds: "Now, one of the groups with whom I meet is a multiracial group in which people have a greater socioeconomic diversity. I sense a greater ability to firmly test one another in ways that don't threaten the core relationships. I believe that race and class are key reasons for this difference."

After determining whom to invite and extending the invitation either to particular individuals or a larger group, the next step is to let people know what a faithfulness group involves. It can be helpful to hold an introductory meeting in which people learn about faithfulness groups and the kind of commitment that might be required. Before this meeting, distribute copies of the guidelines or make this book available. You may encourage people to watch a video about faithfulness groups. (See the resource list for more information about guidelines, videos, and other helpful resources.) At the introductory session, it's good, when possible, to have one or more people speak about their experience participating in a faithfulness group. Leave time for questions and answers.

At an introductory session, it can also be helpful to give people a taste of what it's like to talk intimately with another person about their inner spiritual life. One way to do that is to invite everybody to engage in the following exercise with a partner. In pairs, people speak about some aspect of their spiritual life, then listen to their partner. For example, each person could speak to the prompt, "Tell me about a recent time when you experienced the Spirit at work in your life or when love caused you to take action." The job of the listener is to be lovingly, nonjudgmentally present, without commenting or questioning, just listening and waiting in silence, whether the speaker is talking or pausing. At the end of five minutes, the two people change roles. The listener becomes the speaker for five minutes. After this sharing, it might be helpful for the pairs to take two minutes each to describe to one another their experience of sharing and listening about the spiritual life. Then the group as a whole can have a conversation about that experience and how it relates to the kinds of sharing and exploration that are done in faithfulness groups. It is important to remind people that the details of what other people have shared are confidential and not to be repeated.

After this introductory opportunity to experience what is involved in faithfulness groups, it is time to form a group of people committed to participating together in a group on a regular basis. Four to six people is ideal, but the process can also work with three people. The group needs to decide upon a time, place, and frequency for meeting. Once a month for two hours is a good basic plan. The group may commit to meet a certain number of times, perhaps four or six times (so each person has an opportunity to be the presenter at least twice) and then decide whether or not to commit to ongoing meetings.

In order to begin to know each other in a deeper and more spiritually intimate way, some groups may want to get together for a meal and have a time of mutual sharing about their faith journeys before commencing the faithfulness group format at their second meeting. Before the first meeting, participants may also want to listen to a recording of a faithfulness group session to gain a better sense of the focus, atmosphere, and kinds of questions to ask.

Making a commitment to regularly attend meetings of the faithfulness group is important in helping the group and its members develop spiritual intimacy and meet the invitation of the Spirit into a powerful place of spiritual encounter together. One participant writes, "Keeping the commitment to meet regularly matters. [So does] being understanding that occasionally things happen and an absence here and there can't be helped."

Practices for Faithfulness Groups

The following practices are useful during faithfulness group sessions. Some, such as deep listening, are so essential that they are used in every session. Other practices, such as appreciating inner images, are used less often. Not all of these practices will be used by a group when it first begins working together. Over time, groups grow as the Spirit leads them in their time together, and additional practices may be incorporated.

Deep Listening

Deep listening is a foundational practice. A faithfulness group can only do its work to the extent that members attend to the words, experience, and presence of other members of the group and at the same time pay attention to the presence of the Spirit among them. Listening is often used as a metaphor for a kind of sensing that happens not only with spiritual ears but also with inner vision and spiritual heart. This deeper kind of listening helps us be attentive to the movement of the Spirit within ourselves, others, and in the world. It allows us to become increasingly sensitive to the promptings of Love and Truth. For most of us, this kind of listening is not easy because it requires us to still our own thoughts and preoccupations for the sake of being open to God.

Western culture has a long history of denying and discrediting the inward voice of the soul, of the Spirit, and of God. Most of us have learned, consciously and unconsciously, to do this. Therefore, divine guidance may register in our consciousness only in very fleeting, subtle ways. However, as we pay attention to subtle inner impressions, it becomes easier to perceive the voice of the Guide. We learn to value inner images and knowings and to heed guidance when it comes.

We can practice giving attention to the divine voice when we listen to another person speak about their spiritual experience. In doing so, we help the speaker also attend to the subtle divine presence within them. This is a precious gift we can offer, a skill worth developing. As Quaker author Douglas Steere writes, "To 'listen' another's soul into a condition of disclosure and discovery may be almost the greatest service that any human being ever performs for another."[4] This kind of listening helps a person hear and speak inner truths they may not have previously disclosed even to themselves. In order to listen in this way, we need to let go of our distracting thoughts and give clear, open, nonjudgmental attention to the person who is speaking. When we are listening, it is sometimes helpful to tell ourselves that in this moment nothing is more important than paying attention to the speaker.

As we listen, we don't frame a response. We don't analyze or interpret what the person is saying. We just listen. We listen to the words and the meaning they are trying to convey. We listen to the quality of the speaker's voice, to the feeling or passion in what they are saying, or, alternatively, to the restraint we might hear in their tone. When the speaker pauses or stops speaking, we may feel an impulse to fill the silence with words. A response might come quickly to our mind or a similar story, affirmation, interpretation, or advice. In some situations, these can be helpful, but in a faithfulness group our intention is to help the presenter listen to the inner Guide, which will lead them if they can hear it.

We provide an accepting silence in which significance can be explored, motivations tested, and truth revealed. Deep listening helps the speaker hear the truth within them. Loving receptiveness can help another person listen to themselves and to the Spirit in a deeper, more trusting way than they have experienced before.

Sometimes in the midst of speaking, or at the end of giving an answer, the speaker becomes silent, turning their attention inward. In the practice of deeper listening, when the presenter is paying attention inside themselves, we don't fill the silence with any words. Instead of asking a new question, we keep silent. We "hold the space" for the experience that is taking place inside the presenter and watch to get a sense of what is happening within them. They may be experiencing communion with God, praying, listening for guidance, or remembering something important. Prayerfully, we hold them in the Light.

Into this receptive silence, the speaker may offer something else. They may say something they have never articulated before, revealing a new truth. More often, they may give voice to something they have already said, but by saying it again in this group they can allow more space inside them for the truth of it. Often, the practice of repeating certain inner truths helps something bloom in a person's consciousness and in their life.

Deep listening is a powerful spiritual practice. This kind of listening is related to discernment, in which we learn to sort out what is coming from a divine source and what is coming from another source. As we listen to another person in a loving, receptive way, attending to the truth of their souls, we become better able to listen to our own souls. We become more sensitive to the voice of the inward Guide, the voice of God within us.

After having had deep and moving experiences in a faithfulness group, one participant advises, "Listen, listen, listen—to the sharing that is offered to us, and to the inner voice of Spirit as we hold the pain or joy or confusion or hope, or whatever it is that each of us brings to our sharing." Our intention in providing this kind of listening is to support the presenter in a deeper exploration of the truth in their heart and to help them grow in their relationship with God. Listeners will often find that exercising the loving discipline of deep, patient listening brings blessings for them, too.

Looking at God and Sensing the Presence

Whatever names we use for the holy Mystery from which life arises, faithfulness begins with turning toward God. Some people have experienced the divine Presence since childhood. For some, the theology in which they were raised was adequate for understanding the nature of life. Others have had experiences that awakened them to divine reality in unexpected ways and gave them a hunger to know the Spirit more deeply and more frequently. We may not know what we are turning toward. We may have rejected our family or our culture's prevailing notions of God or Christ and only know that we are seeking something greater or more loving than what we have known.

We may turn toward God with longing or love, or with fear, anger, confusion, or desperation. Whatever we are feeling, whatever questions we have, we are invited to bring all of ourselves to God, just as we are. A faithfulness group helps its members do that.

When we use the word faithfulness, we may think of acts of boldness and courage, of public witness, or of hidden sacrifice for the benefit of others. All of this is often part of a faithful life, but faithfulness begins quietly in the heart and mind and soul, in direct relationship with the Divine. Spiritual growth comes from placing God (Spirit, Christ, the Light, divine Mystery) at the center of our attention and allowing God to love us, heal us, guide us, and act within and through us. Our role in a faithfulness group is to support each other in the process of reorienting our lives so that God is at the center. Growing in faithfulness involves learning to sense the subtle work of the Spirit within ourselves, in others, and in the events of our lives. We can help each other do this by repeatedly inviting each other to "look at God" or at least to "look for God."

How can we help each other do this? By creating invitations to remember and speak about experiences in which we had a sense of the presence, guidance, or activity of God (or Spirit) or felt deep Truth or Love moving in our hearts. We listen when one of these precious experiences is shared. Then, as prompted by the Spirit, we can ask the speaker to look more deeply at what happened, to savor the experience, and to sense how the Spirit was at work in that moment. A listener might ask, "Say more about how God was present with you then." Or, "In that particular moment, what was happening inside you?"

In addition to asking a presenter to remember and look more deeply at a particular past experience, we can also invite them to pay attention to an experience unfolding in the moment during the group session. We can ask: "What is your sense of the presence of God with you in this moment?" Invite the person to stop thinking about anything and just notice what is happening inwardly right then. If they say something like "I'm feeling a tingling" or if they have a sense of fear or of energy moving, it might be helpful to ask, "Where are you feeling that in your body right now?" Our bodies are capable of communicating information not only through our physical senses but also through our spiritual senses. In a faithfulness group, we can gently invite each other to tune in to these senses.

Because speaking about such perceptions and experiences has usually been discouraged in our culture—even ridiculed or punished—a person may have been suppressing their awareness of the movement of the Spirit for a long time. They may find it

31

difficult to respond to questions about what they are sensing in the moment. In that case, the imagination can become a doorway through which they learn to perceive what is real. A listener might ask, "If you imagine a loving God with you now, what would that divine loving parent want to say to you?"

Responding to these prompts to "look at God" or "sense the Presence" and speaking aloud about the experience can feel risky. Over time, two kinds of trust develop. The first is that the speaker begins to discern and trust what is real, even when the imagination is used as a doorway for exploration. The second is that the speaker learns to trust the group to be unconditionally, lovingly present with them as they explore their spiritual perceptions and experiences and then speak about them.

Making a conscious decision to put God or Spirit or Love at the center of our lives and to let the divine Presence motivate our actions is an important turning point in life. But our deeply ingrained habits of putting other things at the center are not quick to change. We require lots of practice in turning toward God, again and again. Participating in a faithfulness group provides an opportunity for regular practice with the support and encouragement of others. The questions we hear from fellow group members sometimes become ones we ask ourselves in our lives outside of the group. One participant finds herself "asking some of the questions we ask each other when I am looking for clearness. 'Where is God in this? Can I feel God's Love for me in this? Am I being faithful? Have I prayed about it?'"

Asking Evoking Questions

When offering spiritual support and assisting with discernment and faithfulness, questions are asked not to satisfy the curiosity of the questioner but to help the presenter become more aware of the truth about the issue they are exploring. Rather than asking for facts or analysis, it is especially helpful to ask evoking questions, questions that assist the focus person in exploring their deep responses and inner knowing. Factual information and analytical reflection may be useful in understanding a situation, but a different kind of awareness is often needed in order to become clear about the interior movements of the Spirit. Questions that evoke greater awareness help free the presenter to live most fully and authentically. Such questions seek to elicit the knowing that may lie below consciousness or that may not have been articulated out loud before. They invite the person to use their imagination and to describe images, metaphors, feelings, sensations, and bodily awareness. Some questions ask the focus person to "look at God" or to sense how God is present with them, both in the moment and in the situations and concerns upon which they are focusing. Faithfulness groups create a space for inward listening on this level and gently encourage the focus person to speak aloud their emerging awareness.[5]

When framing a question, it is important to notice the spiritual language the focus person has been using. Does the focus person speak of Jesus as their guide and teacher or as their savior? Do they use the word God or do they speak of Spirit or the Light—or something else? Upon occasion, it is helpful to ask a question that probes the person's theology or spiritual language, a question that invites them to test their direct experience alongside the words and images they use to find what is most true. Often, though, it is best to use the language that is most comfortable to the speaker.

Below are some simple examples to illustrate the difference between factual questions, questions that invite mental reflection and analysis, and evoking questions that invite a deeper kind of knowing or awareness of how the Spirit is leading someone.

Distinguishing Evoking Questions from Factual or Analytical Questions

Example #1

Chris is led to do a particular piece of writing and is seeking to find the heart of it.

Factual question: How long do you want this article to be?

Analytical question: What do you think your audience wants?

Evoking questions:

- What's your sense of what God may want to communicate through this writing?

- What image do you have for how this writing may affect your audience?

- What aspect of this topic do you feel most passionate about?

33

- Is there any aspect of your own life that you sense this writing is calling you to reexamine?

- Is there a story, movie, poem, or Scripture passage that comes to mind related to this?

- Have you had any dreams that might be connected to this piece?

Example #2

Jess is discerning about a possible leading to take a particular job.

Factual question: When would you start?

Analytical question: What skills would you need compared to your current work?

Evoking questions:

- How do you sense God's presence in this opportunity?

- When you imagine doing this work, how does your body feel? What happens to your breathing?

- Have you received any hints, messages, or signs about this possibility?

- As you imagine taking up this work, do you have an image of how you might be challenged to grow?

- What gifts might be drawn out of you by this service?

- How do you feel when you think about who you would be serving?

- Does this opportunity feel like a temptation? If so, why?

- Do you feel a sense of duty in relation to this? If so, where does that sense come from?

Sometimes a response suggests that something significant might emerge if a follow-up question invites the presenter to further explore some aspect of what they have just said. Be attentive to the focus person to see if this is needed before a new line of questions begins. A follow-up question may be asked by a different group member than the one who asked the original question.

Examples of Evoking Questions for Use in Faithfulness Groups

Modify the following questions for the specific needs of the moment.

What seems most to help or hinder your attentiveness to God?

How do you sense God at work in you or through you when you are seeking to serve?

How do you listen for guidance?

What do you experience when you pray about what God is asking of you?

What are your experiences and assumptions about what prayer is, how it happens, and the power it has?

What images or phrases or Scripture passages seem to be sources of guidance for you at this time?

How much freedom do you have in responding to the promptings of Spirit?

Do you seek God's help in addressing your impediments to faithfulness? How?

What might allow you to trust and relax more in your efforts to hear God's guidance and be faithful?

How is God working with you in this? What are you learning?

What fears are coming up? What resistance are you experiencing? Can you pray about your fears or resistance?

As you look at particular moments when you feel that you were used by the Spirit to serve others, what do you notice about the presence or activity of God?

What is the stretch or growing edge into which God may be beckoning you right now?

How willing are you to enter into the unknown, to do new things or speak in different, clearer ways?

In which situations do you feel you are most authentic and faithful to what you were most truly made to be?

What are the signs of grace you have seen in your service?

What help or support do you need from others in being faithful to how God is calling you?

As you take steps in faithfulness, what opens up in you and outside of you?

Opening Ourselves to the Light

Growth in the spiritual life requires continually opening up to the transforming Light and healing love of God. As we gradually learn to put God at the center of our awareness and our lives, we see more clearly how Spirit infuses everything. Our personal burdens become lighter when we let God help us carry them. At the same time, we also become more aware of parts of ourselves that are hurt or contracted. These things have often been hidden below our normal consciousness. Whatever has been injured or narrowed, everything within us that is angry, afraid, jealous, or resentful, becomes illuminated so we can see it more clearly. Both in ordinary moments of daily life and in our devotional time, when we encounter pain, fear, anger, resistance, or an unsettling memory, we can "show it to God" or "hold it in the Light" for God's healing. We can also help the members of our faithfulness group do the same.

Most of us avoid pain and fear when we encounter them. We have developed habits that push aside unpleasant feelings. We seek distractions, including entertainment, conversation, engaging with the internet, excessive eating or drinking, and busyness. As a way of distracting ourselves from deeply feeling our pain or discomfort and sensing the roots of it, we often mentally analyze or complain about our difficulties or blame others. On the spiritual path, we learn ways to directly face our inner injuries and limited or false beliefs and open ourselves to healing. Prayer, journal writing, loving relationships, counseling, mindfulness meditation, and physical or energetic healing practices can be helpful.

The faithfulness group has a role to play when members discover that a hurt, contracted place or fearful belief is an impediment to a person's faith and faithfulness. Many people are deeply burdened by shame or by low self-esteem. When they receive inner nudges toward certain tasks or hear inner spiritual guidance to speak out or do things they have never done before, internal voices of shame or low self-worth may tell them they are mistaken about their spiritual leadings. It is not the group's role to engage in a psychological analysis of the issue. Rather, with gentle questions the group can invite the focus person to sit with what comes up and "show it to God" or "hold it in the Light."

Inviting God to be with us as we turn our attention to difficult things is a step toward healing injuries and releasing false and limiting thought patterns. It can also be a step in the process of forgiveness. When we hold something in the Light or lift it up to God's care, we are first of all allowing ourselves to give nonjudgmental attention and awareness to the impediments to our faithfulness. The group's loving attention can help us remember to be kind and loving to ourselves and remind us that God loves us unconditionally and wills our peace and well-being. When we "show" the hurt or fearful parts of ourselves to God, or hold them in divine Light, we invite divine love and healing to enter more fully into what has been hidden, contracted, or defended.

Our awareness of the presence of God within and among us may be so subtle that we rarely notice it. Being together with others in our faithfulness group, prayerfully and patiently focusing on God, can heighten our awareness. Rather than merely suggesting that a person take time at home to engage in a direct encounter with God, we can encourage them to do so in the moment, during the faithfulness group session, if the focus person is willing. As group members develop trust and spiritual intimacy, this becomes easier. When one person takes the risk of engaging directly with the Spirit during the group time, the group becomes a safer place for others to do the same.

It is not only our pain and fear that need to be held in the light of God's love. Each of us also has spiritual gifts and potentials that we have not yet fully actualized. Because of painful past experiences, limiting beliefs, or negative self-concepts, we may have learned to keep our gifts and potentials largely hidden, even from ourselves. A faithfulness group can help us not only to see why we hold back these potentials but also to identify what these gifts are. Because we may have kept them hidden for a long time, it may be painful to acknowledge them, to "show them to God," to "hold them in the Light." After we begin to admit to our gifts, then we can sense more clearly how we might be called to use them. Sometimes our fear becomes stronger at this point because using our spiritual gifts will mean being different than we have been and, therefore, facing new reactions from people. It may be scary, but this kind of change calls us into greater freedom to be who God created us to be. A faithfulness group gently helps its members to sense and acknowledge their abilities and potentials that have been held back and to discover how the Spirit might want to work through their gifts.

Sometimes tears come when a person reveals something that has been hidden or suppressed, or they may come during an experience of showing God a hurting place inside or acknowledging a gift that has been held back. These tears are part of the healing and opening process and don't need to be stopped. It might be helpful to silently place a tissue nearby, but don't distract the person from attending to what is happening inwardly.

The spiritual companionship provided by a faithfulness group can allow us to reveal ourselves in new ways, speak of deep and previously hidden spiritual longings, and open to spiritual perceptions and senses that have been closed. One participant writes of an experience in one of his early faithfulness group meetings:

> I was speaking about my longing for a deeper connection with the Spirit, and I found, as I responded to questions from Friends, that I felt liberated to feel the experience of longing in a different part of my heart and my being. It was as if I had been invited to open a door that required the assistance of others to open, and that only the connection that we had formed together in this effort of mutual love and seeking allowed me to secure their assistance in the way that I needed. I felt as if I was talking . . . from different ground.

Another faithfulness group participant remembers a transforming moment she witnessed in her group:

> A person was in the middle of a major life-change that was not of their choosing. Through our listening, questions, and worship together, we were present as a challenge was

embraced as an opportunity to go deeper with God and to put God, not life circumstances or other people's opinions, at the center.

One day, during a meeting of my own group, I spoke about the painful feeling in my heart that constrained me in certain situations when I was speaking about my spiritual experience with others.

"Can you show that to God?" a member of the group asked me.

Although the tightness in my chest was familiar, I had not considered "showing" it to God. Now, the circle of friends around me was inviting me to feel my pain, fear, and contraction in their presence—inviting me to look at it and see what was going on and, at the same time, to open the situation to God's healing.

It was an opportunity to be with them in a way that felt vulnerable and risky, right then and there. That day, I was able to accept the invitation. Because these friends had gained my trust, I allowed myself to be raw and vulnerable in front of them. I felt my pain and fear. Tears slid down my cheeks, and I closed my eyes. In my mind and heart, I lifted the situation up; I "showed it" to God. There was a long period of silence.

"What's happening between you and God right now?" the same person asked.

I was inviting God into this knot of contraction. I felt my sadness and pain, my sense of being alone and in danger in certain situations when I was trying to be faithful.

As I sat quietly showing this to God, I suddenly felt a shining flow of divine, compassionate love entering into my heart. Something was released. A layer of constriction fell away. Suddenly, I felt lighter, freer, tenderly joyful. The room seemed brighter. I felt love for the friends who were sitting with me. That day, with their simple, gentle questions, deep listening, and prayerful attention to the divine Presence among us, my faithfulness group facilitated a kind of spiritual surgery. In the faithfulness groups I have been a part of over the years, I have experienced many spiritually liberating moments of awakening, healing, and renewal. Each one is part of my gradual rebirth into the person God created me to be.

Prayer and Worship

Faithfulness group meetings begin and end with prayer and worship. Sometimes the convener offers a verbal prayer at the beginning of the meeting, either a spontaneous prayer or one previously composed. Whether or not there is vocal prayer, most of the prayer time is in silence. Each group member looks within for the presence of God—Christ, the Holy Spirit, the Inward Light—and gently lets go of thoughts and concerns that distract attention from a focus on the Spirit. In the silence, as group members look within, they begin to be gathered together by God into a deeper place of spiritual attention.

During the presentation by a focus person, group members listen attentively, lovingly, and without judgment. Over time, we learn to stay in a state of prayer while listening and also during the period of evoking questions and deeper exploration. The entire meeting can be experienced as a time of unbroken prayer and worship. Faithfulness group meetings give us an opportunity to notice when we shift out of the state of prayer into another state. Mentally analyzing what the presenter has shared can move us too much into our heads, and then we forget to focus on the Spirit. We may forget that the focus person's inner spiritual Guide can lead them into the clarity they need. If we remain in a prayerful state, responsive to the work of the Spirit among us, God will make use of the gifts and perceptions of the group members to find the right questions and loving remarks to help presenters find their path forward.

Sometimes we are prompted by the Spirit to encourage prayer in the moment. Presenters often share the troubles they face, not only inner difficulties but outer obstacles that are put in their way. At other times, they might share weariness or a feeling of deep soul sadness. Group members might be prompted to ask, "What happens when you share that burden with God?" Such a question is a reminder that turning to God in prayer is always helpful. Be careful, however, to phrase the question in a way that is an invitation to exploration rather than a disguised suggestion.

The focus person might be ready to share their burden with God in the moment, in the midst of the group session. He or she might become quiet and inwardly invite God to help them hold or face the situation. It is healing to feel—not just mentally "know"—that God is with us in our difficulties. For some people, there is a physical sense of well-being or inner warmth that may accompany a sense of being in God's presence. On some occasions, the burden may become lighter in the moment. One participant writes that in her group she has seen someone who was carrying a heavy load "brighten . . . when asked if they might try to share the load with the Spirit."

Over time, group members learn that the most powerful way to assist each other during faithfulness group meetings can be by deeply and prayerfully attuning together to the Spirit within and among them. Sometimes silent prayer for and with the presenter is what is most needed; at other times, spontaneous spoken words of prayer can be a blessing. When the group is gathered into the Light in a powerful way, that power can gradually effect changes in each person long after the meeting is over.

Appreciating Inner Images

Images are a more primary language for the soul than words, and for many they are an important way to receive inward spiritual guidance. Some inner images that come in prayer, meditation, or dreams contain great wisdom and truth. If contemplated, they may assist in needed transformation or healing or provide guidance leading toward a new way of doing things, a service that may be required, or the best possible future. Simply focusing on an image and allowing it to affect all of one's inner senses can help a person receive the wisdom, healing, and transforming power the image conveys. When such images arise within, a faithfulness group can help its members notice and savor them.

A focus person may use a metaphor in a striking way and even repeat it as they speak. If so, it can be fruitful to invite them to look more closely at the image the metaphor offers. It is good to phrase this invitation as simply as possible, without adding any interpretation. Avoid complicated suggestions, which can distract the focus person from their interior exploration.

"You spoke about a door opening for you. Could you say more about that image?"

"I notice you repeated the phrase 'hard as a rock.' I wonder if you could say more about the image of a rock and what it feels like to encounter that kind of hardness."

"When you told us your dream, I was struck by the image of the little girl running through the spring meadow. What happens when you focus on that image?"

The following are examples of appreciation of an image. The first example is personal and the second is that of a friend.

Primeval Forest

Several times, during moments of great inner stillness at the morning meeting for worship at Pendle Hill Retreat Center, I have had an impression of being in a primeval forest, unspoiled, wild, and natural. My deep interior silence was accompanied by a sense of awe. I felt surrounded, supported, and sustained by the ancient forest to the core of my being.

When I explored the image, I felt a holy power and a sense of great fertility, of unlimited possibilities. The image reminded me that the land on which Pendle Hill stands was once unspoiled forest inhabited by the Lenni Lenape people. But the primeval forest that I sensed was older even than any human inhabitants. It existed prior to human beings.

When I recollect this primeval forest, the image has the power to help me touch into the state I experience in a deeply gathered silent meeting for worship with others. The holy, original forest is a metaphor for the Ground of Being, the fertile matrix of all life that we call God. The Ground of Being is a pure state of consciousness, undisturbed by fear, greed, alienation, or attachment. Recalling this image helps me connect to a sacred state of oneness with God and with all things, a state that contains great healing power and unlimited potential.

Warmth and Rainbow Light

A friend of mine has received much support and insight from an early memory. In this memory, he is around two years old, a barefoot toddler walking onto a porch lit by the morning sun. The floorboards under his feet are pleasingly warm. More pleasing is the light that falls on his feet as he walks into the room. Bands of rainbows are reflecting from the edges of the window panes. When he lifts his foot to step on a rainbow, the rainbow appears on the top of his foot. It is magical.

This memory of warmth and magical rainbow light comes to my friend from time to time. He believes it has shaped his consciousness in an important way by leading him on some deep level to always be ready to step into something unexpected and holy. Sometimes he uses the image in his prayer for others: "May they be filled with warmth and rainbow light."

Exploring Dreams and Visions

In Scripture, God, the Holy Spirit, or "messengers of God" sometimes communicate with people using words. For example, after Elijah fled for safety into the wilderness and was sleeping under a bush, an angel touched him and spoke. Later, after he reached a cave in the sacred mountain Horeb, he heard a gentle whisper, "a still, small voice," the voice of God speaking to him directly, asking him, "What are you doing here, Elijah?" When Elijah answered, he received some very specific instructions.

Today, many of us expect to hear from the Spirit in words, but receiving divine guidance in the form of clear verbal instructions is relatively rare. Spirit communicates in many ways. Those who do not pay attention or accord importance to images, visions, and dreams can miss divine messages intended for them.

In both the Hebrew and Christian Scriptures, the Spirit communicates through dreams. Sometimes it is not clear whether an experience is a dream or a vision, that is, whether or not people are asleep or awake when they receive images that provide guidance. In Numbers 12:6, God says, *"When there are prophets among you, I the Lord make myself known to them in visions; I speak to them in dreams"* (NRSV). Numerous prophets were guided by dreams, and others who were not called prophets also had dreams containing divine guidance or foretelling possible future events. Joseph, the husband of Mary, was guided by God several times through dreams. Another Joseph, one of the twelve sons of Jacob, was guided by powerful dreams and also had a gift for interpreting the dreams of others. Ananias (an early Christian in Damascus), the Roman centurion Cornelius, and the apostles Peter and Paul were all guided by dreams and/or visions.

Though they may offer helpful insight, most dreams do not contain divine guidance. It is necessary to exercise discernment about what dreams are revealing. Nonetheless, for many people, paying closer attention to dreams or to the images and visions that come during prayer or at other times may prove to be an important way to receive divine instruction. Sometimes a single dream or vision can provide unfolding guidance over many years or throughout a lifetime. Often, the dreams containing such guidance have a luminous quality or a sharper sense of being real than other dreams.

It can sometimes be helpful to bring to one's faithfulness group a particular dream, vision, or image received in prayer. There are many ways to help each other better understand the spiritual significance of dreams and the truth or guidance they contain. However, working with other people's dreams is not the primary goal of the faithfulness group. As with all other material shared by a presenter, the task of the faithfulness group is to help the focus person explore the significance of dreams and images for themselves, particularly as they relate to their connection with God and their efforts to be faithful. With open, evoking questions, groups can help each other access the inner knowing that indicates when they have come to a true understanding of the guidance they have received.

Noted dream expert Jeremy Taylor always insisted that all dreams come in the service of health and wholeness. His work with many thousands of people from communities around the world made him certain that dreams operate simultaneously on many levels. Therefore, they can communicate or reflect multiple truths about the dreamer and give guidance related to more than one aspect of life. Even if the dreamer has found an understanding of a dream or vision that rings with deep spiritual truth, additional insights may come later. Certain luminous dreams or images may continue to give fresh guidance as a person's life unfolds and they confront new challenges or follow fresh leadings.

Even small fragments of a dream can contain important guidance. Taylor tells the story of a student in one of the seminary courses he taught. Training to become a pastoral minister, this student could never remember a dream to share with the class. Finally, when pressed to share anything, one day he admitted that maybe his dream the previous night had contained "pastel colors." After many questions that evoked no insight, a fellow student asked: "Is there any association in your mind between the word pastel and the word pastoral?" The dreamer had an important "aha" moment. He admitted that his commitment to the "pastoral life" of being an ordained minister was "distinctly pastel," or pale. He realized that he had enrolled in seminary in order to fulfill his parents' ambitions for him but that he was not finding it a path he could commit to with passion. The realization of this soul truth changed his life in dramatic ways, and he left seminary. Later, he became a leader in another type of community.[6]

Mirroring

We can serve as mirrors for the other members of our faithfulness group, lovingly reflecting what we see in them and thereby helping them to see themselves, their gifts, their leadings, the truth within them, and their relationship with God more clearly.

We can do this with brief observations and gentle, nonjudgmental questions. We might ask the focus person, "When you talked about that possibility, I heard joy in your voice. Could you say more about that?"

Instead of "I heard joy," we might say, "I heard fear," "I noticed excitement," "Your face glowed," "I heard passion," "There was anger in your voice," "Tears came," etc. Or, we might simply ask, "Could you tell us what was going on inside you at that moment?"

It is best to state what we see as directly and clearly as possible and in few words. If we use lots of words, it is likely that we are projecting something of ourselves onto what we are describing in the other person. The longer we speak, the more we may distract the focus person from paying attention within themselves.

Because most of us have had long practice, since childhood, discrediting or muffling the still, small voice of God within us, we often doubt the reality of the spiritual guidance and leadings we perceive. When members of a faithfulness group sense the genuineness of these leadings, they can help reflect this back. It is important not to simply affirm everything the focus person says; all group members have the responsibility to discern the movement of the Spirit. Sometimes it is appropriate to briefly reflect back the divine presence when we sense it, to say something like "I sense God at work in that" or "There is a ring of truth in what you just said."

When we don't hear that ring of truth, we can invite the focus person to explore more deeply. "Is there something you are afraid of here?" "What is your sense of the presence of God with you as you look at the situation that way?" "Where does that inner voice come from?" Helping the focus person to sort out for themselves which motivations and impulses come from social conditioning or old hurts and which have the ring of divine truth is a great gift we can give.

One faithfulness group participant who constantly questions whether or not her actions spring from a true leading finds the support of her faithfulness group very helpful: "The group confirms my actions as Faith-based when I am almost always in doubt."

Another way we can mirror what we see is to help each other, through evoking questions, see how God or grace is at work in the situations and events of our lives in ways we had not noticed before. One participant's faithfulness group helped her reframe something she had been experiencing as an affliction. The group helped her to see that "having this affliction allows me or can allow me to understand others who have a similar affliction and to support them and care for them with greater empathy." It is wonderful when we can help each other see things in the light of God at work within us and among us. We must be careful, however, not to simply press our views about this onto another person. It is better to ask open, evoking questions that help each person sharpen their own perceptions. We might ask, for example, "How might God be making use of this affliction?" Or, "Tell us about the empathy you feel for others who experience the same condition."

Finally, a very important way that we serve as mirrors for each other is by revealing our longing to be intimate with God and our desire to be faithful. Those who show this to each other through open, vulnerable sharing reflect these same qualities in the other members of the group. As we reflect back and forth the presence of the Light within each of us, that Light brightens in our midst.

Mutual Accountability

Each one of us has a role to play to participate in the divine plan for healing humanity and the earth. The ways we are asked to do this and the actions we are called to undertake often challenge our sense of ourselves or disrupt our comfortable habits and ways of being. God calls us to be humble, courageous, truthful, loving, generous, and bold.

It is normal to experience fear and resistance when led to faithfully speak, act, and live in the ways God asks us to do. We have already looked at how a faithfulness group can lovingly help members acknowledge their fear and resistance and ask the Spirit for help in freeing them. More than that, when people reveal the truth of their calls and leadings, the group can later help them remember the clarity that emerged and help them keep facing the obstacles to their faithfulness. When a person habitually doubts their gifts or ability to follow the leading of the Spirit, the group can help them look deeply and honestly at their spiritual potential.

Society and culture exert enormous internal and external pressures upon people to conform to the status quo. Groups that have taken an alternative stance from the majority view or behavior can help members live in ways that are different from the culture. But most alternative groups, even religious groups, are still embedded in cultural assumptions, biases, and practices more deeply than they know. People may believe themselves to be filled with the Spirit and faithful yet still conform to cultural practices and ideals that are contrary to the ways of God. These include a materialistic orientation; a culture based on greed, racism, xenophobia, and oppression of other people in distant places; the disruption of the climate; and the destruction of the planet's ecology through behaviors considered ordinary and normal by society, such as burning fossil fuels for transportation and heat and cutting down old-growth forests for lumber. To become open to how God may ask us to change the ways we live and to invite or help others to do the same, we must practice humble vigilance, knowing that we are all struggling to have the courage to hear the fullness of God's call.

In exercising mutual accountability, we hold up possibilities for each other that may seem impossible and we help each other remember that we are called to newness, courage, and an abundant life beyond what we have known. One faithfulness group member wrote, "I recently was encouraged through the questions of others to honor a leading to speak something that felt like it was of God. I needed to overcome great reluctance and fear to speak, and it took a full year for me to act on the message." She explains, "My faithfulness group has helped me keep my feet to the fire, if you will. Through years of gathering together, I am constantly reminded of both the opportunity and need to move from thinking about a leading to praying. I have also been encouraged to serve the Divine in a variety of ways and to better prepare for this service."

Some people use the faithfulness group as a place to focus on a particular call or leading they are following. Each time they make a presentation to the group, they invite group members to help them look at how the Spirit is leading them, step by step, in following their leading or living into their call. It helps when presenters actively invite the group to help them understand any obstacle they face and to look at any resistance or fear that is holding them back.

Noting how difficult it can be to follow a leading that attempts to change the way things are, one participant wrote, "I can't imagine engaging in ministry which deeply challenges the status quo without the support of a mutual accountability group."

Spontaneity and Experiments

For some people, the schedule and format of faithfulness groups seem too rigid at first. It can feel awkward or annoying to be reminded of the clock when someone is sharing deeply and intimately. Over time, however, it becomes clear that the schedule allows a kind of freedom. It provides a structure in which profound exploration, healing, and transformation can happen, yet it remains a format that works for members with busy schedules. Over time, moving from one thing to the next at certain intervals feels more natural, part of a flow. The format and schedule create fairness, too. In the long run, each person gets equal time, and the group does not have to agonize at every meeting about whether or not to give extra time to one person and less time to another.

Although the sequence and timing are set, faithfulness group meetings allow room for the movement of the Spirit, for creative questions, spontaneous prayer, and moments of grace. Sometimes a group member will feel a prompting to ask an unusual question that may seem to be "out of the blue." It's wise to inwardly test the prompting—is it really from the Spirit? If so, then ask the question and see if it opens a new exploration or awareness for the focus person.

Sometimes the Spirit will prompt the group or one or more members to speak aloud words of prayer for the focus person or to offer them the opportunity for hands-on healing prayer, if that seems right for them. Occasionally, it may seem right to set the schedule aside altogether and allow the focus person to ask for whatever help they need during their session time. This may happen, for example, when a person scheduled to present is faced with an unexpected and shocking life change such as the death of a loved one, the loss of a job, or a tragedy. Maybe they just need to speak at length and then be held in prayer rather than be asked questions.

Some groups follow the suggested format most of the time but leave open the possibility that, upon occasion, the presenter may feel led to ask to use the time in an uncustomary way. One group regularly welcomes diverse ways of using the presentation or discussion time. A participant in this group wrote:

> We have assisted one another in looking at strategic directions, priority goals, followed up on intentions from prior sessions, and shared resources related to our focus topics. Sometimes the fifteen-minute time has been used to share materials developed for a presentation to a group, to review the annual report of a ministry, . . . [or] to consider the implications of a grant proposal on a potential project. While we generally use the process as the container, we allow the content to transmute as best serves Spirit and one another.

She continued, "I believe that it is critical that we refuse to constrain the forms, tools, and leadings involved in spiritual accountability. Spirit blows where it will; might we follow?"

Love

> Love is above all, and when it prevails in us we shall all be lovely and in love with God and one with another.
>
> —William Penn

Love is the most important gift faithfulness group members offer each other. As hearts open and trust develops, love flows. In a faithfulness group, love sometimes emerges at the very beginning, even before members know each other well. Listening to people reveal themselves and speak their deepest truths in an open and vulnerable way opens the hearts of the listeners and allows profound spiritual love to enter in. It has been said that God is love and that where love is present, God is present, too. Faithfulness groups often experience the truth of these sayings.

One participant wrote,

The familiarity and trust that my faithfulness group has developed with one another has allowed us to speak very openly about difficult personal matters and about our relationship with God. These are not conversations that I regularly have with other people, but I have found myself able to speak more clearly about my spiritual life and my spiritual aspirations with other members of meeting and with some members of my family.

He added,

We have learned to be more silent with one another, to slip more easily into worship, to invite God into our worship more readily, to trust in our and each other's ability to hear, love, heal, delight.

Another participant described three ways that participating in a faithfulness group helps her be more faithful: "Setting aside the time to seek faithfulness in the presence of friends who do likewise; learning to listen to Spirit's guidance; seeing myself through the loving eyes of friends."

Participation in a faithfulness group has helped another person discover that a spirit of love is hidden within everyone: "I have become spiritually intimate with others in a new way, and have come to believe that a spirit of love is within us all but is often deeply hidden."

The love that can flow in a faithfulness group meeting comes through the hearts of those present, but it is not a personal love. When hearts are opened, it is above all God's love that flows into and through the group. This divine love has tremendous power to heal, guide, and change the members of the group and, through them, to reach more deeply into the world to heal others. Each time a group meets, it is possible for hearts to gently open more widely than before, helping group members learn to become more and more willing and able to be channels for the Great Love that wants to heal all of humanity and the earth.

When God Does Something Unexpected: Simon Peter Meets with a Faithfulness Group

According to Scripture, the Apostle Peter did not ask others to join him in discernment after the events described in Acts 10 (and recounted again in Acts 11). Scripture does not say how he knew that the extraordinary vision he had and the voice he heard were from God and the Spirit. The following is an imaginary account of what might have happened if Peter had taken his experience to a faithfulness group and asked for help with discernment.

For the sake of exploring what a group session might be like when dealing with a challenging discernment, let's imagine that Peter has come to his faithfulness group to tell about the vision described in chapter 10 of Acts of the Apostles. His group already knows that Simon, now called Peter, was a devoted disciple of Jesus of Nazareth and was among those who received the outpouring of the Holy Spirit in the Upper Room on Pentecost. Peter is a leader in the newly forming community of the followers of Jesus. He has been traveling to share with fellow Jews the good news about Jesus. Now he wants his faithfulness group to help him interpret a puzzling vision he had and discern whether he should accept an invitation to go into the household of a high-level Roman officer.

In our imaginary faithfulness group session, Peter explains that while staying in Joppa at the home of Simon the tanner he went to sit on the rooftop while the household was preparing the midday meal. He was hungry. Under the hot noonday sun, he drowsed off and had a vision in which God lowered a sheet from heaven containing many kinds of animals. Peter's imaginary faithfulness group members know that, according to the laws of the Torah, the only types of meat that may be eaten are cattle and

51

game that have "cloven hooves" and "chew the cud." Other animals are considered impure; faithful Jews are forbidden to eat them. The animals on the sheet included ones that were deemed unclean, possibly pigs or camels.

God spoke to Peter.

Get up, Peter; kill and eat. In this vision, God was asking him to do something contrary to the laws about kosher food. Peter's first response was to refuse.

Absolutely not, Lord! I have never eaten anything impure or unclean, Peter answered.

The voice rebuked him. *Do not call anything impure that God has made clean.*

God's command posed a dilemma. Scripture forbids the eating of such animals. How could God be asking Peter to do something contrary to what is written in Scripture? Which should he obey—the voice of God or the words of Scripture?

The vision repeated itself. The sheet was lowered from heaven to Peter on the rooftop, and again the voice of God told him to kill the animals and eat them. Peter responded with the same refusal, and he heard again the same rebuke: *What God has made clean, you must not call profane.* For the third time, God lowered the sheet holding the animals. Peter gave the same response, and the voice chastised him again. Suddenly, the sheet with the animals disappeared and Peter was awake, puzzled by what he had just seen and heard. Had he really just received instructions from God? Was it possible that God had asked him to do something that is forbidden in Scripture?

The members of Peter's imaginary faithfulness group would probably have been puzzled, too, and even distressed. Most likely, some would have felt certain that God would never ask anyone to do something contrary to what is written in Scripture. Some may have wondered whether Peter was seriously stressed out from all that had happened lately. Was it possible he had gone out of his mind?

But Peter's experience did not end there. He tells his group that as he was puzzling on the roof about the strange vision, he heard the voice of the Spirit speak to him again.

Look, three men are searching for you. Now get up, go down, and go with them without hesitation; for I have sent them. Peter went downstairs and greeted three strangers who had just then been asking for him at the gate outside the house. One was a Roman soldier, and the other two were servants of the Roman centurion Cornelius. They told Peter an extraordinary story. Cornelius, considered by those who knew him to be a good and righteous man, was also very devout. He gave charity to the poor and prayed continually to God. One afternoon, an angel appeared to him in a vision and spoke his name. Terrified, Cornelius asked the angel what he wanted. The angel replied that his prayers and his acts of charity had touched God. The angel instructed Cornelius to send men to the town of Joppa to find a man named Simon, called Peter. These were the men who were now at the gate. They had known where to find Peter even though he had just recently arrived in Joppa. They explained their mission.

Cornelius, a centurion, an upright and God-fearing man, who is well spoken of by the whole Jewish nation, was directed by a holy angel to send for you to come to his house and to hear what you have to say. 7 This invitation, like the vision that had immediately preceded it, posed a dilemma for Peter, because Jews did not enter the homes of Romans, whom they considered impure and unclean. Furthermore, it was Peter's understanding that the message of Jesus was only meant for Jews, not for gentiles.

In spite of their surprise and wonder, the imaginary faithfulness group has listened quietly to Peter's presentation and his questions. When his presentation is finished, group members ask one or two very brief clarifying questions. Then they take some minutes of silence to pray about it. Many feel a great deal of intensity as they ask the Spirit to guide them in their questions and listening so they can help Peter discern whether his vision came from God or from some other source. Was it just a reflection of his hunger and his inner confusion and stress? Were the dream and the visit from the Romans temptations to do something sinful? Probably they all feel it would be safest to advise Peter to ignore the vision and refuse to go to the centurion's house. On the other hand, the group members want to be faithful, and they know that God's ways are sometimes mysterious.

"Please help us as we help Peter discern about this!" they are praying in the silence.

They know that it is not their job to tell Peter what to do but to help him discern what comes from God's spirit as opposed to any other source.

"Peter, what happens when you pray about this?" one of them asks.

"I don't have a clear sense about it when I pray," Peter says. "But I have the feeling that this is something very important, and I can't just brush it aside, even though I want to. In my prayers, I keep telling God that I don't want to do anything he forbids. And I keep hearing the words, '*Do not call anything impure that I have made clean.*' I don't know if he is talking about eating pigs or going into a home of Romans, but both of those things seem repulsive to me. How could I do either? I tell God this doesn't make sense. But then, when I keep praying about it, it seems like God is saying to me, '*Behold, I am about to do a new thing; now it springs forth, do you not perceive it?*'"

The group waits in silence for a few moments. They look around at each other to see who has been given the next question.

"Peter, when you hear those words from Scripture, '*Behold, I am about to do a new thing,*' what do you feel in your heart?"

Peter remains silent for a little while.

"I feel a strange warmth," he says.

"Anything else?"

Peter closes his eyes, and the group waits quietly.

"Now I remember that Jesus said to me, '*Feed my sheep.*' Could there possibly be some good Romans whom Jesus wishes to bring into the kingdom of heaven? Is it possible that God wants me to go into that household? Why did an angel appear to Cornelius and tell him where to find me and then order him to send for me? Has God made these Romans clean?"

Several members of the group feel the temptation to discuss or debate these questions with Peter, but they remember that their job is to help him sense the true leading of the Spirit for himself, from within. Silently, they look around at each other. One of them has been holding a question, and this seems like the right moment.

"Peter, is there something familiar about saying 'no' to God three times?"

"I'm very stubborn," Peter says, and he laughs. Then he thinks about it some more and the group waits in silence, watching Peter's face change.

"It happened the night Jesus was arrested," Peter says in a low voice. "I said 'no' three times before the cock crowed. I lied and said I didn't know him. I was so afraid." Tears slide down his cheeks.

"Are you afraid of what might happen if you go into the centurion's house?"

"If God wants me to go and I don't, I'm afraid I will disobey and disappoint him. If God doesn't want me to go and I do, well, I'll be a fool and a sinner."

"When you think about the things that Jesus said and did, in relation to the Romans, does anything come to you?"

The group waits in silence while Peter looks inside himself to see if a memory arises.

"I remember that day in Capernaum when a centurion found him and said, 'Lord, my servant is lying at home paralyzed, in terrible distress.' And Jesus said immediately that he would go to that man's house and cure the servant. He started walking there without any hesitation. But the Roman officer said something like, 'I am not worthy that you should come under my roof. If you only say the word, my servant shall be healed.' Jesus praised the centurion for his faith, and he said that there were some gentiles who had more faith than the people of Israel. Then Jesus told the centurion, '*Go; let it be done for you according to your faith.*' And we heard later that the servant had been healed in that very hour" (Matthew 8:5–13).

In our imaginary faithfulness group session, Peter remembers that moment when Jesus had commended the Roman officer's faith. But then he thinks about the terrible oppression of the Roman occupation of Israel and all the injustice he has seen. He has witnessed humiliation, brutality, and many terrible crucifixions. Very recently, Jesus had been horribly scourged and then crucified alongside two others.

"How many times must we forgive?" Peter asks his group with anguish. They sit with him, feeling the terrible pain of oppression and praying to God.

Finally, Peter speaks again, his head down.

"Do you think God loves even the Romans?"

Everyone in the group is silent, praying for clarity about what God is asking their friend to do. Finally, Peter lifts his head and looks around to see who will ask the next question.

"Peter, when you were guided by God in the past, what did that feel like?" someone asks.

"After Jesus left, I felt a commission to share the good news. It was like a yoke had been placed on my shoulders. I was no longer free to just go anywhere I wanted. In fact, ever since I first became a disciple, I have felt that I needed to follow Jesus and go where he went. This week, it seemed clear that I needed to come to Joppa."

"When you imagine going to the house of Cornelius, do you imagine Jesus going with you?"

"I feel his spirit with me now."

"If you imagine walking with those three Romans to the home of Cornelius, what comes to you?"

"Before he left, Jesus told me that I would sometimes have to go to places I did not want to go."

"Do you feel like he wants you to go with those men?"

Peter sits with this question. He had wanted his faithfulness group to tell him the answer, but he knows he has to find it inside himself.

"Maybe this is what God meant when he told me to eat animals that aren't kosher," he responds. "Maybe the good news is meant for all, not just for Jews. Maybe this is the new thing that God is doing."

"Peter, how does it feel when you say that?"

Peter is trembling.

"I feel the power of the Spirit is at work in this."

The other members of the faithfulness group feel it, too.

The Fruits of Faithfulness Groups

Faithfulness groups can revitalize the faith of individuals and communities. By attending to the work of the Spirit together, groups help their members sense and tap into the divine love and guidance that is always available. As each person gains greater openness to divine love and guidance, they radiate encouragement to others. Numerous faithfulness group participants have testified to the renewal of faith among their members, people who have, in turn, become beacons of the Light for others. One participant described the effects of his deepened spiritual intimacy with members of his community. He had attended weekly worship with some of his fellow group members for decades but had not known the depth of their inner lives:

> My faithfulness group has welcomed me into the spiritual lives of close friends and members of [my Quaker] meeting in a far deeper way than I had previously experienced. I have been profoundly moved and completely surprised by some of what I have seen and learned, particularly the ways in which Friends are in communion with the Divine. This experience has been an inspiration to me, and it has allowed me to open myself more fully to the activity of God within me. . . . I am reminded that my companions in this search, while plagued by doubts and insecurities similar to mine and while often dealing with significant personal difficulties, maintain an active and vital connection to the Spirit. I am still amazed and inspired by this, and I am encouraged to be more faithful. . . . I suspect that over time the connections our faithfulness group has created, and the manner in which we have created them, will radiate more fully through our [Quaker] meeting.

Another group member has been deeply nourished by the love she receives in her faithfulness group. Over time, her participation in the group has deepened her spiritual understanding. Her faith community, recognizing this spiritual ripeness, nominated her to serve on their worship and ministry committee, an appointment she accepted:

> Unconditional love for each other is the #1 way we support each other. After that, deep listening; knowing we are seeking to be open to the presence and movement of the Spirit in our questions and response to the focus person. . . . Knowledge of experiences and concerns that the person has brought to us in the past sometimes informs our understanding of now. That depth of knowing one another helps us grow in faithfulness, strengthening our trust of one another; I know that the others in the group know me. That is sustaining. . . . I believe that the faithfulness group increased my spiritual depth and faith, and perhaps as a result I was asked to be on the worship and ministry committee. I bring love and knowing about seeking discernment to that committee.

Members of long-term groups report that participating in a faithfulness group sharpens their ability to discern and follow the promptings of the Spirit, grows their faith, and leads them into profound Love.

Another person wrote that the fruits of nurturing the faithfulness of individuals is helping her Quaker meeting, as a whole, grow as a spiritual community in hopeful ways:

> I think that our meeting is in the process of developing into a true spiritual community, for the first time since I have been part of it—twenty-two years. This is a fragile work in progress, but nevertheless is in progress. The meeting has had fleeting moments of being a gathered community in the past, but this is a sustained, organized effort.

People who have participated in faithfulness groups describe many other fruits of the practice. Below are thoughts on some of these other fruits, grouped by topic. These comments come from participants in many different faithfulness groups.

Greater Awareness of Self and Others

> I have loved being in a faithfulness group, I have felt closer to Spirit and closer to my authentic self because of the love and attentiveness of people in my groups, and I have seen

deeply into others' processes in seeking and following faithfulness.

In the same way that surround-sound adds to one's experience of a film, being able to witness others in their faith walk provides me with a diversity of perspectives about how Spirit moves in our lives. Our shared practice reveals ways that I am different from and similar to others and they me.

More Tender and Compassionate toward Others

I hear firsthand about the movement of the Spirit in the others in my group. I am more tender toward others, including those I disagree with, as a result of this regular opportunity to put God at the center.

Increased Ability to Speak with Others about Faith

Participation in a faithfulness group was helpful in overcoming embarrassment about taking about spiritual matters (something I did not grow up with), and the practice (and the nonjudgmental listening of the members of the group) led/enabled me to have greater facility in finding words to explain non-concrete experiences.

Because of my Faithfulness group . . . I began to understand 'faithfulness' better and have been able to speak about it more easily in my meeting.

Support for Spiritual Practices

The faithfulness group is an excellent tool for maintaining your spiritual practices and spiritual life.

Deepened Sensitivity to the Spirit

The group offers me an opportunity "out of time" to focus deeply on Spirit and its movement within myself and within our group. It has deepened my awareness of Spirit in my life and has allowed me to be more sensitive to Spirit on a day-to-day basis. I am awed at every meeting at how we go to ever deeper places each time, whether we are sharing joy in our calling or struggling with a dark patch in our journeys. Participation with this group has also helped me be sensitive to Light/Spirit as it operates in the lives of others, even others who are not part of this particular group of seekers.

Greater Awareness of the Spirit in All Aspects of Life

[The faithfulness group] deepened my awareness of the movements of Spirit in my life—through paying closer attention and speaking aloud.

I feel the connection with others who experience the movement of Spirit more quickly and more fully in my dealings in both my meeting and outside in the business and social realms. I believe I have become more sensitive, somehow, to that of God in other people, and live from a place where I can honor this more fully in my interactions with others.

I find that I am in an attitude of worship far more often than I was before my participation in my faithfulness group.

Growth and Transformation in the Spiritual Life

[Participating in a faithfulness group has] shown me how we can all get stuck in long-term mental ruts and, yet, we can also break out of them with Spirit's help using our peers as a conduit.

I have been able to talk to my [Quaker] meeting about my spiritual journey and I will be speaking to a meeting I attended in the past about why, after thirty years, I became a member of the Society of Friends. I would not have had the courage before . . . [participating] in my faithfulness group.

One member of our group struggles profoundly with trusting the wisdom that God has gifted to her, as she travels through a very difficult personal and employment transition. We have all watched her open up to that wisdom and seen grace break in for her, moving her toward finding peace with the inner guidance that is there for her. Her questions to us, as each of the rest of us share our journeys, have become insightful touchstones in important ways to each of us; and this seems to be springing from the transformation she is undergoing herself.

Faithfulness groups are in practice a combination of deepening faith and then being able to use that strengthened faith for the next step in the outer world. . . at least it has been that way for me. . . or clearing away the obstructions to seeing where spirit is leading. As a member of our individualistic culture, it took me awhile to understand that this was something intended to be productive beyond my own egoistic concerns.

Support for Living a Faithful Life

There have been a number of times that I have tested the direction of my work with Spirit through the group and found direction both large and small concerning future actions. . . . It has helped me continue in my ministry position. Without having peer support I might have resigned due to isolation.

Currently, at a time of waiting for a clear path, the group helps me have faith in waiting and in seeing that of God in the work I am doing now.

I recently chose to sign up for a class that will last for more than a year partly as a result of my faithfulness group. I have also done better preparation for following leadings as a result of my participation.

I believe I had a call or leading prior to being in the group, but this refreshed my commitment and made it feel more communal. I am not on this journey alone—easier to remember my guide and be faithful to it. [My faithfulness group is] an external reminder and motivation for me to be faithful, gives me comfort and love in the course of my spiritual journey, and helps me with insights into the state of my spirit.

I have seen the Spirit at work so strongly in the lives of people who have been in my faithfulness groups as they followed leadings to spiritual work. Their leadings were nurtured by the group and often became a clear path of service for these individuals. Their leadings and ministry then nurtured other Friends, their meetings, the Society of Friends, and the world. I believe the support of the faithfulness group, when a member hit roadblocks and disappointment associated with following their leading, was important in providing love and support for the person in the face of disappointment.

Expanded Sense of the Call to Ministry in All of Life

Recently, I saw how the teaching ministry in a programmatic way had morphed into a real-time, on-the-ground form of spiritual accountability. Theory gave way to practice, not in a group that agreed to meet for a specified amount of time regularly, but in the larger faith community of which I am a member. Just as accompanying another in ministry . . . [is] far more revealing, real, and enspirited than simply hearing the minister's account of it, engaging spiritual accountability in real time has been much more challenging, more fraught with opportunities to err, and more public. At the same time, the potential for Spirit's presence feels far greater in those places, the potential for impact on people's lives more real, the probability of effecting meaningful change in the world far more likely. It is the movement from learning to knowing to teaching to practicing unceasingly.

Going Deeper with Faithfulness over Time

Faithfulness groups, like individuals, go through stages in their ability to help each other listen for God's call and respond faithfully. Most groups begin with energy and enthusiasm for the new enterprise. At the same time, beginning groups often experience some awkwardness accommodating to the focus and guidelines of the group. There can be difficulty, for example, if one or more members find it hard to refrain from giving advice, interpreting another person's experience, asking questions motivated only by curiosity, or telling their own stories during another person's focus time. These problems and others can be addressed on the spot by someone calling gently for a time of silence or reminding the group of the guidelines. They can also be identified during the time of assessment at the end of each session. When group members learn to give honest, loving feedback about how well they are adhering to the group's intention and guidelines, they discover over time how to use their faithfulness group meetings to more effectively go deeper into the life of the Spirit. Whenever a new member is added to the group, the whole group needs to go through a process of reminding each other and teaching the new person how to maintain an atmosphere of holy accompaniment and focus on the faithfulness of each focus person in turn.

Gradually, as the members of a group grow to trust each other and reveal themselves more authentically and vulnerably, the group learns to enter more deeply and more often onto Holy Ground. It becomes easier to ask, hear, and respond to hard questions. However, even though a group's overall movement is toward deeper trust and intimacy with each other and the Spirit, there can be times of dryness and superficiality in the life of the group, just as there are in the lives of individuals. Sometimes people come to the meeting feeling overburdened or very tired. Sometimes there can be a sense of sleepiness and resistance to deeper exploration. A group may have a tendency to shield their members from taking the risks of complete faithfulness. It is helpful to notice this and be curious about the causes. Compassionately exploring the reasons can lead to helpful insights and make possible a deeper kind of faithfulness for all members of the group.

As a group becomes disciplined about the focus and atmosphere of their sessions and more experienced in helping one another deeply explore God's leadings and their responses, they become better able to discern when something different from the recommended format is being prompted by the Spirit. A focus person experiencing a significant crisis, for example, may not be able to give a focused fifteen-minute presentation. They may speak more briefly or need a longer time for others to simply listen without asking questions. A period of focused prayers, whether silent, verbal, hands-on, or some combination, may be the best way to support the faithfulness of a particular focus person. Sometimes the group may discover that the best way to support a person's faithfulness in a particular session may be an exploration involving physical movement or something else outside of the norms. Some groups are led to develop their own alternate norms over time.

It is common for groups to lose a member over time and to invite another person to join them. Such changes can be beneficial. Without it being noticed, a group that has been meeting for a long time without change may develop subtle patterns of relationship that hinder their openness. Attachment to the group may make members hesitant to support leadings that would take a beloved member away from the group or move them in a direction that might challenge everyone. If the members of the faithfulness group belong to a larger group, such as a Quaker meeting or a particular congregation, they must exercise care in how they speak to each other or about the group in the larger setting to avoid creating an exclusive clique or making others feel excluded.

Although some groups include only people who are sharing a common type of leading, such as prison ministry, most groups include people whose calls and leadings are varied. Over time, some overlap may develop. One member of the group may feel led to provide certain kinds of support or accompaniment to another member beyond that provided within the group meeting. For example, one person in the group may have a leading to travel to offer a message about climate change, economic justice, or spiritual healing, and another member of the group may sense that they are being led to travel as a spiritual companion to the first person. The sense of having a leading to accompaniment can be explored and tested in a faithfulness group session.

Over time, a group may grow in awareness that even though its members are following very different leadings, there is an underlying spiritual connection between them. They discover that the faithfulness of each member of the group somehow serves to nurture the faithfulness of the others in a hidden or underground way.

On rare occasions, a group may discover that all its members are given a leading to carry out together. That could be something as simple as sharing information about the faithfulness group practice with other members of their community. Or, it could involve a call to a much larger and more complex undertaking.

A Friend in a long-running faithfulness group had been living for a long time with a sense of following a leading. With the support of an oversight committee from his Quaker meeting, he had traveled to speak and lead workshops among Friends with a letter of endorsement from his meeting. But, at some point, the call to that ministry seemed to end and the oversight committee had been laid down. In the next few years, he experienced challenges in his meeting's community and changes in his work life. During those years, the subjects he brought to his faithfulness group related primarily to discerning a faithful path through these changes. As the group helped him explore how he was being led by the Spirit, they got glimpses of a new, deepening way that God was calling him to travel in the ministry among Friends, visiting other Quaker meetings to share a message. Questions were offered that helped him pay more attention to the deeper current, and he started exploring it more fully when it was his turn to be a presenter. This was hard to do, however, because he became aware that God had laid a burden on him, the call to convey a message that most people did not welcome hearing.

At a meeting when it was his turn to be the presenter, this man spoke about the burden he felt. He answered the group's questions but seemed to be holding back, speaking about the leading as though from a distance. After one presentation, someone asked what it would be like if he gave as much time and

65

attention to this leading as he had been giving to addressing a health concern. At the next meeting, some in the group felt that they needed to find a way to encourage him to speak from within the leading rather than speak about it in a detached way. A group member invited him to share the message he was being asked to communicate. Finally, the man began to speak the message directly. The energy, passion, and truth were palpable. It became clearer to the group why the message would be difficult to deliver and also why it needed to be spoken. Soon afterward, he asked his Quaker meeting for a clearness committee to help him discern the new direction that his ministry was taking. Several months later, after a clearness process, his meeting recognized his call to travel among Friends to share the message and wrote a letter encouraging other Quaker meetings to invite him to visit and speak with them.

The Potential of Faithfulness Groups

Human beings are created with the capacity to be filled with divine love, to live in harmony with God's will, and to be dedicated to contributing to the greatest good that is possible. We have spiritual senses that can tune us into the loving guidance and energizing power of the Spirit. Faithfulness groups encourage their members to greater boldness in listening and responding to God's call. For many, this results in a greater willingness to speak truth clearly and an increased ability to love, forgive, and serve others. Some people find they are called to make radical changes or to take great risks for the sake of manifesting God's love, truth, and justice. A faithfulness group can make God's work possible by supporting the careful discernment of such a call and helping members make required changes and take the necessary steps. Often, the support and participation of many is needed for faithfulness to become possible.

In our time, we are being called to shed our overemphasis on independence and to focus more on life lived deeply with and for each other. In faithfulness groups, as we open authentically to each other and more trustingly to the divine Presence, we soften our hardened, self-protective boundaries and discover more fully the greater love that unites us with one another in the wholeness of God. Quakers have often had the experience they refer to as a "gathered meeting" in their meetings for worship, an experience of collectively being drawn into a deeper union with one another in the Spirit. This experience can also happen in the silences and prayerful accompaniment of a faithfulness group. Together, members learn to sense the Spirit and hear more clearly the truth of God's guidance for each and for all. The more people practice this skill with each other, trustingly and whole-heartedly, the better able they are to access this state in other situations and with other people, including the wider group of their faith communities. Faithfulness groups cultivate capacities that are growing in the human race and that can become more accessible to all.

In the twenty-first century, we are living in a time when humanity is facing unprecedented changes and challenges. Rain forests are being destroyed, and the polar caps are melting. The sea is warming, killing plankton that provide the oxygen we breathe. Pesticide use threatens the lives of bees necessary to pollinate much of the food we eat. As global temperatures rise, more and more arable land is turning to desert, and forest fires are becoming more intense and difficult to control. Reports released by the United Nations and by the United States government predict an acceleration of climate changes that will likely bring about devastating economic, agricultural, and social collapses if not checked. Drought and war have already created a large number of refugees. The predicted flooding of coastal cities will displace a great many more people globally. The climate-related changes already underway and predicted for the future present a greater threat than humanity has collectively faced since the last ice age, when our numbers were much smaller and people were more mobile. The threatened changes are so formidable and require us to change in such significant ways that most people prefer to avoid facing them as long as possible. Humanity continues the behaviors that have contributed to these climate changes and even intensifies them, such as by engaging in more extreme and dangerous means of extracting fossil fuels rather than pouring needed resources into the rapid development of clean sources of energy. We continue to build huge houses for single families rather than developing on a large scale the modest and communal ways of living that will be needed for our collective survival in the future.

The Creator of this world, who animates our sacred planet and who lovingly abides within each one of us, wants to lead humanity to a hopeful future. Times of crisis can call out dormant potentials. In our time, human beings are invited to evolve into a new level of being, to live in conscious awareness of our oneness and in joyful cooperation with the divine love that wants to act through us to bring healing and newness. Faithfulness groups (by whatever name) have a crucial role to play in supporting people to open to the creative, loving, healing work of the Spirit within and through us.

In certain periods in history, it is exceedingly difficult for individuals or groups to go beyond the norms of their times. But at other times, the winds of the Spirit can move powerfully through groups of attentive, faithful people who mutually support each other. It is possible for human beings to waken from the trance of cultural norms, cultivate spiritual sensitivity, and work together to create societies that encourage a new way of life on earth. In our time, this can happen more rapidly than ever before and on a wider scale. It is possible for humanity to live into a hopeful future as we face the enormous challenges and changes that are present and coming in our time. In faithfulness groups, we can help each other activate potentials of the Spirit that we did not previously believe were possible, abilities to receive divine knowledge, to heal, and to connect with other people and the planet on deep spiritual levels. There is great evolutionary potential in small groups of people meeting regularly to help each other pay attention to the Spirit, waken to the presence of God, fully incarnate the Light of Christ within, and take the leaps of courage and faith that will help us move in the direction of the new and renewed ways of living to which we are being called.

Glossary of Quaker and Other Terms

care committee

A group of people that meets on a regular or irregular basis to care for the practical or spiritual needs of a particular person, group of people, or situation.

clearness committee

A group of people that meets one or more times to help an individual, couple, or group of people discern about a leading of the Spirit. Clearness committees are regularly appointed to consider a person's application for membership to the Religious Society of Friends or to meet with a couple who wish to marry. Clearness committees are also used to help with discernment about many other sorts of leadings. If the leading relates to the business of the monthly meeting, the committee will usually be appointed by the meeting. If not, an individual, pair, or group can organize a clearness committee for themselves.

concern

A divinely-inspired sense that one must pay attention to a particular situation that is out of order, and be ready to take action, if so led by the Spirit.

Friend

A Quaker. A member of the Religious Society of Friends.

gathered meeting

A meeting for worship in which many or all of the participants experience a sense of being gathered together by the Spirit into a palpable spiritual unity. There may be a special quality to the vocal messages during such a meeting, a sense that they are all pieces of a larger whole, coming from a divine source. Participants in such a meeting often have the sense that the underlying nature of reality is being revealed.

leading

A sense of being called by God or the Spirit to carry out a particular course of action. A leading often arises from a concern.

meeting

A meeting is a congregation of Quakers (Friends), the community that meets on a regular basis for worship, business, and other matters. Usually it is named for the place where it gathers (such as Swarthmore Meeting) or for a body of water or other geological feature nearby (such as Clear Creek Meeting). Because it meets once a month to conduct its business, it is often called a monthly meeting. A regional association of several meetings, which meets three or four times a year, is called a quarterly meeting. British Quakers refer to their local congregation as a "local meeting." In Britain, several local meetings gather monthly for the area meeting for business.

Once a year, a larger association of regional Quaker meetings gathers as a single body, called a yearly meeting, for its annual business sessions.

The term meeting is also often used to signify the meeting for worship.

meeting for worship

A meeting in which the participants are all, together, letting go of their personal preoccupations and turning their attention to God, often in silence. One or more participants may be inspired to stand and offer a brief spoken message, if so led by the Spirit. A meeting for worship can be brief or long ("extended"). Meeting for worship is usually held on Sunday mornings, and it often lasts for an hour and closes with the shaking of hands.

meetinghouse

The building in which a monthly meeting or Quaker congregation meets.

ministry

In the most general sense, anything that participates in God's work in the world, any service done in response to the prompting of the Spirit. In Quaker contexts, this word has a range of meanings. During a meeting for worship, anybody can be prompted by the Spirit to rise and offer a message to the group, called "vocal ministry." A call or leading that has been recognized by a meeting is often termed a ministry.

oversight committee

A group of people, often appointed by a meeting, that gathers on a regular basis to hear reports and help with discernment, accountability, and support for a person or group whose call, leading, or ministry has been recognized and taken under the care of a meeting. Sometimes also called an anchor committee or support committee.

spiritual practices or spiritual disciplines

Spiritual practices, also called spiritual disciplines, are practices undertaken in order to create greater openness to the Spirit. Such practices include prayer, meditation, journal writing, devotional or scriptural reading, contemplative walks, and more.

testimonies

The cumulative witness of Friends to the ways that God calls us to live. Originally the testimonies were behaviors that gave evident outward witness to lives guided by God, such as wearing plain clothing and refusing to participate in war. Today, people often speak of simplicity, peace, integrity, community, equality, and stewardship as testimonies. Living according to these principles testifies to the guidance of God as Quakers have collectively experienced it over time. Each person must come to their own experience and conviction about how they are called to give testimony in their behavior to the life of the Spirit.

travel in the ministry

A Quaker who has a call or leading from God to nurture the faith of others, share a message, or give witness often travels in order to carry out their call or leading. Sometimes a companion accompanies them.

Resources for Faithfulness Groups

Books

Bieber, Nancy. *Decision Making and Spiritual Discernment: The Sacred Art of Finding Your Way*. Woodstock, VT: Skylight Paths, 2010.

Bill, J. Brent. *Sacred Compass: The Way of Spiritual Discernment*. Brewster, MA: Paraclete Press, 2008.

Dougherty, Rose Mary. *Group Spiritual Direction: Community for Discernment*. Mahwah, NJ: Paulist Press, 1995.

_____, ed. *The Lived Experience of Group Spiritual Direction*. Mahwah, NJ: Paulist Press, 2003.

Drayton, Brian. *On Living with a Concern for Gospel Ministry*. Philadelphia: Quaker Press of Friends General Conference, 2005.

Fardelmann, Charlotte Lyman. *Nudged by The Spirit: Stories of Responding to the Still, Small Voice of God*. Wallingford, PA: Pendle Hill Publications, 2001.

Farnham, Suzanne G., Joseph P. Gill, R. Taylor McLean, and Susan M. Ward. *Listening Hearts: Discerning Call in Community*. New York: Morehouse Publishing, 1991.

Fendall, Lon, Jan Wood, and Bruce Bishop. *Practicing Discernment Together: Finding God's Way Forward in Decision Making*. Newberg, OR: Barclay Press, 2007.

Harvey, Andrew. *The Hope: A Guide to Sacred Activism*. Carlsbad, CA: Hay House, 2009.

Loring, Patricia. *Listening Spirituality, Volume I: Personal Spiritual Practices among Friends*. Washington Grove, PA: Openings Press, 1997.

_____. *Listening Spirituality, Volume II: Corporate Spiritual Practices among Friends*. Washington Grove, PA: Openings Press, 2009.

Macy, Joanna. *Active Hope: How to Face the Mess We're In Without Going Crazy*. Novato, CA: New World Library, 2012.

McTaggart, Lynne. *The Power of Eight: Harnessing the Miraculous Energies of a Small Group to Heal Others, Your Life, and the World*. New York: Simon & Schuster, 2017.

Palmer, Parker J. *A Hidden Wholeness: The Journey toward an Undivided Life*. San Francisco: Jossey-Bass, 2004.

_____. *Let Your Life Speak: Listening for the Voice of Vocation*. San Francisco: Jossey-Bass, 2000.

Wilson, Lloyd Lee. *Essays on the Quaker Vision of Gospel Order*. Wallingford, PA: Pendle Hill Publications, 1997.

Pamphlets

Brown, Valerie. *Coming to Light: Cultivating Spiritual Discernment through the Quaker Clearness Committee*. Pendle Hill Pamphlet #446. Wallingford, PA: Pendle Hill Publications, 2017.

Grundy, Martha Paxson. *Tall Poppies: Supporting Gifts of Ministry and Eldering in the Monthly Meeting*. Pendle Hill Pamphlet #347. Wallingford, PA: Pendle Hill Publications, 1999.

Knutson, Jerry. *Individual Spiritual Discernment: Receiving, Testing, and Implementing Leadings from a Higher Power*. Pendle Hill Pamphlet #443. Wallingford, PA: Pendle Hill Publications, 2017.

Lacy, Paul. *Leading and Being Led*. Pendle Hill Pamphlet #264. Wallingford, PA: Pendle Hill Publications, 1985.

Loring, Patricia. *Spiritual Discernment: The Context and Goal of Clearness Committees*. Pendle Hill Pamphlet #305. Wallingford, PA: Pendle Hill Publications, 1992.

Schenck, Patience A. *Answering the Call to Heal the World*. Pendle Hill Pamphlet #383. Wallingford, PA: Pendle Hill Publications, 2006.

Wajda, Michael. *Expectant Listening: Finding God's Thread of Guidance*. Pendle Hill Pamphlet #388. Wallingford, PA: Pendle Hill Publications, 2007.

Websites and Online Resources

Center for Courage and Renewal. http://www.couragerenewal.org/.

Faithfulness Groups. 1:01:18. YouTube video. Posted by Marcelle Martin, Sept. 25, 2017. https://youtu.be/1CrHAsQZnik. This is an hour-long teaching session on the guidelines for faithfulness groups and the practice of asking evoking questions.

Hoffman, Jan. *"Clearness Committees and Their Use in Personal Discernment."* Philadelphia: Twelfth Month Press, 1991. tract.6. http://quaker.org/legacy/atlanta/Clearness_Committees_and_Their_Use_in_Personal_Discernment.pdf.

Martin, Marcelle. A Whole Heart (blog). https://awholeheart.com. The page on faithfulness groups on this website contains several resources related to faithfulness groups, including a link to a recording of a sample faithfulness group session: https://awholeheart.com/faithfulness-groups/.

Pendle Hill Retreat Center. https://pendlehill.org/.

QuakerSpeak. YouTube. www.quakerspeak.com.

Releasing Ministry Alliance. releasingministry.org/.

Shalem Institute for Spiritual Formation. https://shalem.org/.

Appendix A: Other Kinds of Sacred and Healing Circles

Many people today are feeling the need for groups in which they are free to express their spiritual longings and leadings in a vulnerable and intimate way. Many have been doing so in Bible study sessions, book groups, religious education classes, workshops, retreats, and prayer groups. For some, however, these opportunities do not provide the ongoing, intimate, and focused support that they long for. Faithfulness groups are a powerful way to meet this need, but there are also other forms of sacred and healing circles that support lives of integrity, faithfulness, and prophetic transformation. Below are short descriptions of some of these.

Group Spiritual Direction (Rose Mary Dougherty)

The mission of Shalem Institute for Spiritual Formation is to "nurture contemplative living and leadership." While Sister Rose Mary Dougherty served as director for spiritual guidance on the staff of Shalem Institute, she developed a format for group spiritual direction in which all participants are committed to "being there for each other in their desire for God." In her book *Group Spiritual Direction: Community for Discernment*, Dougherty describes a group process that involves a commitment of about one year. It begins with a five- or six-hour gathering on the "opening day," during which participants engage in silence and contemplative prayer, discuss the format and shared assumptions of group spiritual direction, listen to each person briefly share about their spiritual journey, and witness and then discuss a sample "real play" of a group session focusing on one person. Subsequently, small groups of four or so meet twice a month for meetings that last about two and a half hours. During that time, each of the members has about twenty-five minutes as focus of the group: ten minutes to give a presentation, a period of silent prayer, and then ten minutes of response from others, including comments and questions. Group meetings begin and end with silence and prayer. At its best, Dougherty says, the group members "experience themselves as co-participants in the Mystery of Love."

The appendix of *Group Spiritual Direction* is a version of the Peer Group Guidelines for Spiritual Directors used in the Shalem Institute's program for spiritual guidance. The format for faithfulness groups described in this book was developed from these guidelines.

Circles of Trust (Parker Palmer)

Quaker author and educator Parker Palmer is the founder of the Center for Courage and Renewal, whose mission is "to create a more just, compassionate and healthy world by nurturing personal and professional integrity and the courage to act on it." The Center's programs are designed to "cultivate the heart and soul of leadership, encouraging people to 'lead from within.'" In his book *A Hidden Wholeness: The Journey toward an Undivided Life*, Palmer describes the Circle of Trust®, a community of two to twenty-five people who meet regularly over a year (or some other agreed-upon span of time) to "create a safe place for the soul" and "support each other on the journey to an undivided life." Members of these groups accompany each other as they learn to hear the voice of their "true self" or soul. In *A Hidden Wholeness*, Palmer describes a community as a "chaotic, emergent, and creative force field that needs constant tending" (p. 76). Circle of Trust groups that are larger than two or three people, therefore, include a skilled facilitator trained in keeping the circle a safe place for the shy soul to reveal itself. Safety is created by focusing on important subjects related to the life of the soul through indirect means, such as exploring a poem, story, or other work of art as it relates to each person's experience. People are invited to speak from their own experience, as moved, and to ask questions about what others share, following the rule, "No fixing, no saving, no advising, no setting each other straight." They trust each person to be instructed and guided by their inner teacher. Circle participants organize clearness committees for themselves in which the other members participate. Over time, these circles develop into communities where participants find wholeness and become better able to live with courageous integrity.

Spiritual Formation Programs and Spiritual Practice Groups

Quakers in several parts of the United States have been offering nine-month programs that include an opening and closing retreat and local monthly meetings of two kinds of small groups. Reading groups meet to discuss readings assigned for that month on topics related to the spiritual life. Spiritual practice groups, usually composed of three to five people, meet once a month to share with each other their experiences as they maintain a regular spiritual practice that they chose at the beginning of the program. Over time, these groups grow in intimacy. Many participants find the experience so helpful and bonding that they continue to meet for years after the nine-month program is over. Many groups go beyond sharing about spiritual practices and spiritual experiences; they support one another in discernment and faithfulness. Quaker spiritual formation programs have been developed in Baltimore, Philadelphia, and other regions of the United States.[8]

Light Groups (Rex Ambler)

Quaker theologian Rex Ambler studied the writings of early Friends to better understand how they experienced being taught, guided, and led by the Light of Christ within. At the same time, he learned the stages in the guided practice called Focusing, created by Eugene Gendlin, which helps people identify an interior "felt sense" of a problem or unresolved situation. Merging these two sources of learning, Ambler created the meditations he termed Experiment with Light, which he describes in his book *Light to Live By*. In many areas of England and the United States, people have formed "light groups" that meet regularly to do the Experiment with Light meditations together and then to share their experiences. Some light groups have met on a monthly or biweekly basis for many years and have developed the spiritual intimacy that enables them to see more clearly how the Light is guiding and leading them. An Experiment with Light network based in England offers many resources online, including guidelines for setting up a light group and a periodic newsletter.[9]

Power of Eight Circles (Lynne McTaggart)

Lynne McTaggart is the author of several books that report on scientific research related to invisible fields of healing energy. In *The Power of Eight: Harnessing the Miraculous Energies of a Small*

Group to Heal Others, Your Life, and the World, she describes the healing effects experienced by participants in groups of six to twelve people who are "open to the possibility of healing and intention." These groups gather on a regular basis, either in person or via the internet. They spend a period of time holding healing intentions for each member of their group and then also for people and situations outside of their circle, including major problems in the world. Her research shows that holding a healing intention—or praying—in groups can have a more powerful healing effect than solitary intentions or prayers. She also reports that many who participate in such groups experience healing effects in their own lives even if they are not the focus of the healing intentions or prayers. Her book suggests that those who hold healing intentions for others tend to expand in their sense of self; this, in itself, opens them to healing effects.

Coaching Circles (U.Lab)

Otto Scharmer and colleagues at Massachusetts Institute of Technology have developed a theory of collective leadership for social change called Theory U. They teach a free massive open online course (MOOC) called U.Lab whose purpose, according to the course description, is to help participants "see the world in new ways and practice a method that allows leaders, entire organizations, and larger social systems to connect with and actualize their highest future possibility." The approach includes spiritual practices but uses secular language. A key element is the U.Lab peer coaching circles. In this format, groups of about five people meet on a weekly basis for seventy-five-minute "case clinics" that focus on a different person each week. The goal is to help "co-sense" and "co-shape" the future that is "wanting to emerge" in the focus person's life. A presentation by the focus person is followed by clarifying questions and then a time of silent reflection in which group members look inside for images or gestures that express their sense of what they have heard in the presentation. Members of the coaching circle then share these images and gestures and the focus person responds. This is followed by questions for deeper exploration, additional responses, or reflections.

Appendix B: Called

This piece describes the process of hearing a call, bringing that call to the attention of the individual's home meeting, testing that call for clearness, and then receiving long-term oversight and support for faithfulness. This Quaker process of discerning and supporting the leadings of God is a way of helping to make manifest the work of God in the world.

This is a revised version of Marcelle Martin's article "Called" published in *Friends Journal* October 1, 2011.

Called

by Marcelle Martin

And the word of the Lord was rare in those days; there was no frequent vision.

—1 Samuel 3:1

"You are being prepared to receive a message." These internal words are accompanied by a shift of awareness to a deep interior place. Around me is a group gathered in morning worship.

Twelve years earlier, in 1984, something had suddenly opened inside me during a year of spiritual searching for the meaning of life. On a night's walk home under a dark and starry sky, I was given a glimpse of a Light permeating and uniting all things in a divine Oneness. The Light was immediate and present in all of Creation, in the distant stars as well as in me. I felt a power flowing through my body and out of my fingertips into the world. I knew intuitively that this great invisible power could heal any problem on Earth.

After that night under the stars, I began sensing that I had been created for a particular task in the world. I recognized that my life was being guided by something far beyond my small human personality, a divine Oneness both vast and universal, more infused into everything than I'd ever imagined from stories I'd heard about God. Subsequent luminous experiences showed me that out of a great love for humanity and Earth, God wants to bring about a healing transformation on our planet. In meditations, dreams, and visions, I saw that as humanity moves toward increasing environmental and social catastrophes and crises, a global shift in human consciousness is needed, a shift to living in harmony with one another and trusting in the direct guidance of the Spirit.

After the first glimpse of the Light that flows through all things, I understood I am called to live my life in conscious daily communion with the Spirit and to teach others how to do the same. This understanding altered the course of my life. At age twenty-eight, having just finished graduate school, I gave up my opportunity for a conventional career path as a college professor, instead choosing to teach part-time while pursuing spiritual growth and sharing what I learned with others.

"You are being prepared to receive a message." Again these words come to me in the morning meeting for worship, and now I feel pulled into an ocean of shining amber Light. I imagine I am being prepared to offer some vocal ministry that morning, a message about being called by God. But I don't know how to communicate what it's like to be asked to give over complete control to God.

I wonder if the Power I am sensing is affecting the rest of the group. Suddenly, the respected elder sitting in front of me pops off his bench energetically and begins to speak. He says that God calls people directly. He recounts the Bible story about young Samuel hearing his name one night. The priest Eli, his teacher, finally understands it is God who is calling Samuel and instructs the boy that if God calls him again, he should say, "Speak, Lord, thy servant is listening." When Samuel listens, he hears a message he must transmit.

The man in front of me telling this story seems to be drawing on the same spiritual prompting I am experiencing, but he speaks with an easiness I don't feel, using a story from the distant past. The message I am being prepared to receive is about what it's like today to surrender control over one's personal choices in order to live for God's mysterious purposes. After the elder finishes speaking, the prompting to speak is gone. Later, I realize that the message I am being prepared to receive is beyond anything I could have said in that morning's meeting for worship.

God Still Wants to Speak and Act through Us

Samuel's story begins in a land where people have stopped receiving direct guidance from the Spirit. During weekly church services when I was growing up, I'd heard biblical stories about prophets, all of them men. The common belief that I absorbed was that prophecy had ended long ago. I had not heard of any contemporary person—man or woman—claiming to hear God's voice. The mystical experiences I began to have in 1984 were, therefore, startling and unexpected.

I sought a spiritual community that could support a person with a sense of receiving divine guidance, and I found a home among Friends. I appreciated the Quaker understanding that we can all be guided by God—women equally with men. In our homes, workplaces, meetings, and everywhere else, we all have opportunities to exercise the ministry of God's love and give witness to truth and justice. I also saw that there come times when individuals and groups experience a leading to dedicate their lives to ministry in a particular way—by taking certain actions, speaking widely about a concern, traveling to be with particular people, undertaking a specific task, or initiating something new.

I found it challenging to make space in myself and my life to hear the subtle voice of God and to live my life in obedience to its prompting. As I paid attention inwardly, I was led toward both inner and outer changes. I needed to spend more time alone or in silence, listening to my heart and using spiritual practices, including prayer, to become more receptive to the Spirit. Outwardly, I needed to let go of a conventional lifestyle, becoming less independent and more communal. I was led to prepare and facilitate courses, workshops, and retreats related to the spiritual life and to offer spiritual nurture to individuals. Sometimes, I was invited to travel. Eventually, I was led to give up my part-time position as a teacher of college writing classes in order to give over my whole life to this ministry. I felt prompted to ask my small meeting to provide support in both spiritual and practical ways. Afraid of making such a request, I wrestled with God about this for months, but eventually I surrendered.

Appendix B: Called

Ministry Belongs to the Community

At a session of the clearness committee appointed to meet with me, a member remarked that I did not have professional qualifications, nor was I charismatic. Furthermore, I had not, in his opinion, obtained enlightenment. I agreed. I had no seminary degree. I was shy. And furthermore, I had not attained a continuous awareness of union with the Divine. However, after much prayer, I told the committee at its next meeting that I felt sure about one thing. For more than a decade, I had sensed God leading and drawing me into this ministry. Many people and groups had testified to being nurtured by it. The task of the clearness committee was not to evaluate me as a professional applying for a salaried position but to discern whether the Spirit of God was calling me. After meeting three times, the committee felt clear that I was indeed receiving a genuine call to share my experience of divine presence and guidance and to nurture others in paying attention to their own experience of God.

To discern whether the meeting was called to support this ministry, meeting members accompanied me to events where I was a speaker or facilitator. I spoke to the meeting about my ministry and answered questions. At a called meeting, Friends threshed many issues, some of them difficult. After eighteen months, the meeting approved a written acknowledgment that I was called to a ministry of fostering spiritual renewal. A support and accountability committee began to meet with me. Some Friends in the meeting and others outside the meeting felt led to offer modest but regular financial support. The difference it made to have this kind of spiritual and practical support was tremendous. It enlarged what I was able to do because I was no longer doing it from a personal initiative; I was doing it as part of a community united in a sense of God at work among us.

Years later, I moved to Philadelphia and became a member of a medium-sized meeting that took my ministry under its care after another eighteen-month discernment process. After fifteen years and another move, I became a member of a third Quaker meeting that also, in turn, engaged in a clearness process and then took my ministry under its care. In all three Quaker meetings of which I have been a member, a committee appointed by the meeting met with me six or more times a year. These groups have been a powerful source of spiritual support and have helped me grow into each new stage as God's call on my life unfolds.

For decades, I have had no regular source of income. I have given talks, taught courses, and facilitated workshops or retreats for Quaker meetings or retreat centers. I served as an adjunct teacher at Pendle Hill Retreat and Study Center in Wallingford, Pennsylvania, and offered courses in my own home. For most of that time, I lived inexpensively with other Friends and did not own a car or have health insurance. I took part-time jobs as necessary. My only full-time salaried employment was during the four years I lived as the resident Quaker studies teacher at Pendle Hill. After that, I took three years to complete a book. Along the way, I worked with others to create and offer several nine-month teaching programs, the first one called The Way of Ministry. The most recent program is called Nurturing Faithfulness.

In addition to these outward activities, I continue daily practices that help me connect more completely with Spirit. In the metaphor of the prophet Jeremiah, my heart of stone is gradually (oh so gradually!) being replaced by a heart of flesh on which is written God's law—a tendered heart that God can guide directly. The Light is slowly, gently dissolving me into itself, and I recognize it as the essence of my own true being. According to the first chapter of the Gospel of John, the divine Light that incarnated in Jesus lights everyone who comes into the world. When my separate sense of self has finally fallen away, I may be able to speak the New Testament words quoted by Christian mystics and early Friends: "It is not I who live, but Christ who lives in me."

Some of my dreams during sleep have drawn on today's technology for metaphors of this inner transformation. In one dream, I can no longer run off of old, run-down batteries but must switch to renewable batteries being recharged by the sun. In a series of dreams, the familiar dented car I'm in stops running; it's time to get out. In the last dream, when I finally get out of the old car, I see a smaller, shining vehicle ahead of me, waiting with open doors. In other dreams, it's time to erase old files and limited programs from my computer. I must shut down and reboot on an entirely new operating system. Jesus waits at the entrance to this new system, welcoming me in.

Called Out by Community

Opening to the fullness of our true identity within the divine Oneness requires the support of a community. Those who are led to particular ministries outside the meeting have felt a strong need for this support. In meetings that have recognized the leadings or ministries of several members, one committee is sometimes appointed to support two or more different Friends. Whether recognized by their monthly meeting or not, some Friends have also formed groups for mutual accountability.

In 2000, I encouraged my new housemate when she, too, heard a call—in her case, a passion to care for the Earth and a leading to teach alternative lifestyles. Her salaried job kept her very busy, but she was so moved by the calling of another member of our meeting that she joined committees to provide support for his ministry. As she witnessed his struggle to center his life in the Spirit, her own leading to do the same gradually emerged. She arranged a demotion at work in order to free up more energy for environmental activism. A trip to South Africa galvanized her sense of urgency in the world, and visits to eco-villages in Costa Rica and Colombia gave her hope that there are ways to choose a sustainable lifestyle and people willing to pioneer that path. Then she accepted early retirement in order to give all her time to the ministry to which she was now ready to dedicate her life's efforts wholeheartedly. For many years, she has been traveling to speak and teach at Quaker gatherings across the country—traveling by bus or train, not airplane or car. She has written articles, prepared PowerPoint presentations, led workshops, and clerked committees.

For many years, she and I were members of a faithfulness group (then called a peer group) composed of six Quaker women. Members of that group created and facilitated religious education and spiritual formation programs, taught about Sabbath Jubilee and the economics of justice, traveled to India to support Quakers and Right Sharing of World Resources work there, ministered among those in prison and in the neighborhoods from which many prison inmates come, wrote plays, and created theater productions that strengthen the soul. We met once a month and focused on two of us at each meeting. We listened, asked questions, drew out deeper knowings and hidden fears, challenged, prayed, cried, laughed, and loved each other. Our struggle, like most women's, included reckoning with deeply embedded social conditioning that denies the sanctity of women. Women of my generation and earlier (and perhaps still today) have been trained to doubt ourselves deeply and to devalue the ideas and initiatives that want to come through us. Faithfulness groups have helped me and others to face and allow God to dissolve layers of fear, self-doubt, and resistance.

I have also participated for more than a dozen years in a group containing both women and men. Sharing my unfolding story and hearing those of others over many years has helped me become more aware of the work of the Spirit and the ways we resist as well as cooperate with it. We all face fierce internal resistance to offering our voices and our actions in the prophetic, countercultural ways to which Spirit calls us.

Both meeting-appointed committees and mutual faithfulness groups help with discernment. In these groups, Friends have the opportunity to speak aloud insights, experiences, and struggles that we have not shared before—or often enough—allowing deep truth to become more fully part of our conscious, lived lives. Through questions and listening, through prayer and encouragement, and especially through love, these groups provide holy accompaniment. As a result, those who participate gradually become more surrendered to God, bolder in faithfulness, and more alive to our call. We are joined with many others in learning how to receive and live into the message that is being given to us to share in the world.

The Need for Prophetic Communities Today

We live in a time of multiplying social crises and environmental catastrophes. Many hundreds or even thousands of species have become extinct in the last century, and the human race may have difficulty surviving the climate changes we have set in motion. Each person and community has a role to play in humanity's choice to evolve to a deeper awareness and find sustainable ways to live on this planet—or not. My mystical "opening" under the stars twenty-five years ago, along with many experiences since then, have convinced me that great spiritual power is available to help us make a huge leap. Realistic hope is still possible if people join together to support each other in being faithful to the divine guidance that can show the way and help us make the significant changes that are necessary.

Before Samuel heard the prophetic call, the word of God was rare and there was no vision in the land. In our time, we have heard the voices of many individual prophets, but they have not been heeded seriously enough. To adequately face the challenges of today, we need more than a few individuals ready to respond to God's call. A bigger miracle is required: groups of people committing to support each other in faithfulness. In our time, prophetic faithfulness will involve more than having an internal dialogue with the Source of all life, more than hearing and transmitting God's words. Like Samuel and the biblical prophets, we are called to speak and act as the Spirit prompts. And even more, we are asked to incarnate the divine Source, to embody it not just in our words and actions but also in our being. Like Christ, we can live as channels of God's Power. Both individuals and communities are called to let the Divine so infuse our consciousness and our actions that we become living embodiments of that great Love that wants to heal humanity and the earth.

Appendix C: Questions of the Grail

In this piece, Viv Hawkins reflects on her experience of peer groups (faithfulness groups), giving an example of how evoking questions by group members helped her explore her difficulties with faithfully following what she was feeling the Spirit asking her to do, utimately freeing her to be faithful.

This is an abridged version of Viv Hawkin's article "Questions of the Grail," published in *Friends Journal* April 1, 2016.

Questions of the Grail

by Viv Hawkins

Jesus uses a grail as a chalice during the Last Supper when he celebrates communion with the Apostles in his last meal before his crucifixion. The ceremony is a way to remember their connection with each other and with the Father. Earlier in his life, he had turned water into wine at the wedding. In his last Passover, wine becomes lifeblood, as the bread (symbolizing the body) is blessed, broken, given, and received—the conditions needed for communion with the Divine.

For more than a decade, I have practiced a peer group model of spiritual accountability that feels to me like a sort of sacrament. Like the grail, the group is a vessel of the sacred in each gathered member and the group as a whole. That communion which holds Spirit—within, between, and beyond us—helps peer group members become more healthy and whole in service to a wounded world.

Each time we meet, our group of four people seeking to be faithful focuses on a slice of the relationship one of us has with the Divine. For a little less than an hour, we sequentially hold the person in prayer; listen deeply as she shares what is present for her; and ask questions that might help her find healing, wholeness, or greater connection to the Holy. The spiritual nurture we share incarnates a message recently offered in [an extended period of] worship: "When many believers surrender together, they are nourished." That is truly a blessing. Yet there is more: not only are we nourished, but we can be nourishing. And we are both as, over the months and years, we co-create, with divine assistance, the sacred container.

Coming together to share our stories of seeking to be faithful— sometimes succeeding and sometimes falling short of what we hope to be or do—we have intimate glimpses into our humanity and our holiness. We offer opportunities to be authentic with others in ways that many people yearn for. We become vulnerable together and lovingly touch tender places and mystery. As at the wedding in Cana of Galilee, water is turned into wine, and life is more festive. Similarly, God is served by people who are focused on faithfulness, on witnessing to the Spirit among us, and on praying and acting to heal our yet-coming world.

During one session, I brought to a peer group my leading to write about spiritual nurture. I revealed my lack of clarity on the leading but explained that I felt invited into an intimate kind of disclosure. Beyond that, I could not see.

In advance of a peer group session, I sifted through several topics that I could write about. I sought one that held particular import for the ministry I carry in fostering faithfulness, one that was fresh and significant in the moment and that felt unanswered. We opened with a period of centering worship to bless the time and to connect with the Holy One. I described my belief that we will co-create heaven when we each follow God's call. I went on to explain my regard for this peer group process as a vessel for faithfulness and my hope to share it meaningfully with others. I then moved on to talk about writing. About 25 minutes into the 35-minute exploration time, Lola referred to me as "prophetic." I became quiet and still. Ivette asked, "What is your heart telling you? Not your head, what is your heart telling you?" I groped for the answer, aided by the Holy within each of us and the collective group.

I responded to Ivette's question about my heart, "There is an invisibility cloak around my heart." Ivette encouraged me, "Stay with that." Accepting her invitation, I sat quiet and uneasily curious, searching within, connecting to that feeling of a cloaked heart, asking myself and God what I needed to uncloak it. After a time, Lola observed, "An invisibility cloak? Sort of the opposite of writing and publishing in a journal; that is not invisible." We left space for God. Nancy inquired, "What is the cloak a symbol of?" I answered, "It is not a symbol of anything. It's hiding the heart. So, at times, when I have felt prophetic, it has been the rebuke of the prophet that I've felt. But rebuking is only half of the work of the prophet; the other half is opening the way for alignment with the Divine."

I continued, "Last year, I participated in a workshop on contemplative photography. We were to notice something and then to be with it for 20 minutes before even using the camera. If I were to use the time well this weekend, 90 percent of it would be used for inviting God to be present. If anything came from it, in any shape or form, that would be the fruit, not the primary focus. How do I remove the cloak to stand in God's presence and hear what is offered?" Other members confirmed the trueness of my revelation.

The peer group, for me, is one manifestation of community joining with God. Until we bless it with our commitment to God and to one another, it contains ordinary wine. But when it is blessed, it takes on a covenantal quality, a celebration of life. Slowly, with each secret part a focus person reveals, with each loving question a member asks, with each prayer we offer up, the blessing is evidence of our mutual accountability with the Divine, and blessings multiply. Over time, we come to better know ourselves, each other, and Spirit's movement in our own and others' lives.

Often in a peer group, what I share feels or is broken. Despite my deep respect for the members of the peer group, my trust in its process, and my faith in God, I'm shy about sharing parts of myself that I wish were more healthy, happy, or holy than they are. Without Ivette's question, I may not have stopped to attend to my heart even in worship or journaling. How often have I seen myself in other people, in areas which were previously hidden and now revealed. Because they had courage or faith in disclosing them, I rejoiced that I am not alone. That, in itself, is a blessing. By acknowledging my heart's "invisibility cloak," I come to accept that part of myself, and am shown that even that part can be loved by others—and, with grace, by myself. When others help me know I am wearing it, I can uncloak.

Giving ourselves as fully as we can to God and to the peer group, and giving each other the space and time to be our fullest selves, without judging, are some of the greatest gifts I know.

We participate in many graces: receiving each person as she is, without needing her to be any different from who she is; receiving God's grace as it flows to us, even when we may not perceive it; receiving from our companions in this journey the gifts they offer. Without these miracles, water remains water and wine remains wine. But with them, together they create both the grail and the communion that we become.

In the end, the time I had imagined available for writing was swallowed up by another project, and seven weeks passed. The day before I wrote these words, I worshiped for three hours with 11 other Friends. We were blessed, broken, given, and received. One part of me floated in limitlessness, and grace offered me a skeleton of concepts for the article I had felt led to write. I came home and put the bones together, then infused it with the flesh-and-blood and breath of the peer group session. This writing is blessed, broken, and given to you with prayers that it may be received, serve, and meet a need.

Viv Hawkins

Viv Hawkins co-founded Releasing Ministry Alliance and studies, practices, and teaches about spiritual accountability. She invites readers to visit releasingministry.org and the Facebook group Friends Spiritual Accountability. She loves Lola Georg, her partner, and carries a ministry to foster faithfulness with a minute from Central Philadelphia (Pennsylvania) Meeting, endorsed by Philadelphia Quarterly and Yearly Meetings.

Appendix D: Holy Accompaniment—The Gift of the Peer Group

The authors of this piece have participated for ten years as members of what they refer to as a peer group, the name used initially for faithfulness groups. They originally met in person. Later, separated by distance, they began to meet once a month by conference call.

This article was originally published May 2017 in the journal *What Canst Thou Say?* (pp. 7–8).

Holy Accompaniment—The Gift of the Peer Group

by Ken Jacobsen, Emma Churchman, Allison Randall, and Marge Abbott

When my wife and life-partner Katharine died this January, the other three members of my peer group asked me if they could come to retreat with me for several days in my now empty house in Wisconsin (on the homestead where Katharine had grown up). I said to them: "Friends, you have accompanied me through so much these nine years of our peer group, joys, sorrows, doubts, fears, disappointments. But this is different—Are you sure you want to accompany now, through death, in my journey of grief, in the hardest time of my life. This is not easy. I might not make it. You might not make it."

"Yes," they said, "We want to accompany you even through death, through grief, in the hardest time of your life."

Appendix D: Holy Accompaniment

I would not wish my condition on anyone, and yet, as I prayed about it, I felt, yes, they should come if they are led. Holy accompaniment is not a half-way, fair weather commitment, it is the sharing of our whole lives with one another in Love.

So we gathered for three days of silence, worship, meals, walks and conversation, in tears and laughter and the whole symphony of emotions. I kept a fire going in the wood stove in the February chill, and I was given the heart to move through another day. I must go through this journey of grief alone, but in the Love with which my peers have surrounded me during these retreat days, I know I am not alone in my aloneness. Thanks be to them, thanks be to the Love that is in them, for Love is of God.

—Ken Jacobsen

A lament of many Quakers who are serious about living a life guided by the Divine, by God, by the Spirit, is that they are unable to find the needed ongoing spiritual support within their home Meetings. Our Meeting might be small, or if it is large there might be plenty of wonderful, good people in them, but these people might not feel as strongly about the importance of God in one's daily life as we do. So we look outside our Meetings, sometimes connecting strongly with someone from our Yearly Meeting whom we see only once or maybe twice a year, or we find a Spiritual Director (usually not Quaker, and therefore perhaps not quite what we yearn for), or someone from a Meeting nearby, or we just keep longing. We four, Emma, Marge, Ken and Allison, were fortunate enough to find spiritual support during a School of the Spirit year-long program.

Nine years ago we took the School of the Spirit course titled "The Way of Ministry." One of the many wonderful things that happened there was that we were divided into groups of four, termed "Peer Groups." These groups of spiritual support and accompaniment met together several times during each of the four multi-day residency sessions that we attended that year, giving support to each person in their ministries. There was a prescribed structure to the time we spent in Peer Groups: Five minutes of opening worship, a presentation of up to 15 minutes by the focus person, a few minutes of brief questions for factual clarification by the other group members if necessary, two minutes of silent prayer and reflection, 35 minutes of deeper questions and exploration. We then got a five-minute break, and the second focus person began the same pattern.

At the start, the members of our group felt rebellious about this: it sounded too constraining, too artificial. But we followed the structure anyway (encouraged insistently by one of our core teachers). To our surprise and relief, we discovered that once we got used to it, the structure helped rather than hindered us.

Something else that we originally thought would be a drawback was that we are such different people, of such different temperaments. (Shaman, nerd, Jesus freak, and Off The Grid). At our first meeting, we never thought this combination of people would work. But it did. After that first residency of three or four days we had already begun to bond.

When over a year's time you unburden yourself entirely to three other people time and time again, talking about what is closest to your heart—your spiritual life, your spiritual challenges—and those people listen with great attention and respect, with their ears, their hearts, their souls, with compassion, and interest, you become very close to one another. Our little group became so close that when the year was over we felt we couldn't bear to end our times together. One of us lives in Wisconsin, one in Oregon, one in North Carolina, and one in New Hampshire, making regular meetings in person impossible, so we decided to meet once a month on the phone, in a conference call. That decision was made eight years ago, and we are still meeting at least once a month.

Our calls are generally two hours long, which gives us enough time for each of the four of us to be the focus person. We begin each call with a short time where one of us expresses willingness to be the convener, and another of us expresses willingness to be the first one to speak out of the silence when it seems right. We then go into silent worship. Unlikely as it may seem, we find that we have deep worship over the phone, probably made possible by the fact that we had that first year of being together in person, worshipping and listening together to God and to one another. When we gather in the silence on the phone and settle into worship we can visualize all of us in a small circle, or as the four directional points. We sink down into the silence quite quickly, feeling unity in the Love that holds us all.

We no longer keep to a strict time schedule. If we discover ahead of time that one of us is in crisis or has some other immediate need and therefore needs more time or the whole time, we agree to that change. Otherwise, under the guidance of our convener we pace ourselves so that at the end of the call each of us has had the time we needed for our unburdening, our speaking, our relating.

At the end of each focus person's time, the convener asks, "what prayer can we hold with you?" and the focus person voices that prayer. We take some time then and there in silence for that prayer, and we each have a little book where we can write and remember each person's prayer. These prayers help us as we hold each other in the Light throughout the next month.

We support one another in our spiritual journeys, have accompanied each other through writer's block, through family troubles, despair, depression, through death and in grief. We have rejoiced with each other in a birth, in publishing of writings, mendings of family difficulties, overcoming of blocks, relief from depression, openings into new life, and so much more. We have come together in discernment, pondering, laughter and tears. We have led workshops together, been elders for one another, buoyed one another up, provided clearness for one another, and called each other to accountability. We help each other find perspective in our interactions with our local and Yearly Meetings and Quaker institutions. We know each other well enough that we can even tease each other, as we notice the same block or problem or concern come up time after time in slightly different guise.

We are four people who are from four distinctly different parts of the country and four different Yearly Meetings, three different time zones, of two different genders, but of one faith.

We are strong spiritual friends who feel great love for one another within that greater Love that guides us.

This peer group is a blessing indeed for all of us.

Margery Post Abbott

Margery Post Abbott is a released Friend under the care of Multnomah Monthly Meeting (Portland, Oregon), North Pacific Yearly Meeting. She has published several books, including *Walk Humbly, Serve Boldly: Modern Quakers as Everyday Prophets*; *To Be Broken and Tender*; and *A Certain Kind of Perfection*. She regularly leads workshops and speaks to Friends groups.

Emma Churchman

Emma Churchman is a member of Swannanoa Valley Friends Meeting (Black Mountain, North Carolina), Southern Appalachia Yearly Meeting and Association, where she serves as clerk of Ministry and Counsel. She is a conscious business mentor, empowering spiritually oriented entrepreneurs to cultivate faith in their business.

Ken Jacobsen

Ken Jacobsen and his late wife Katharine lived and taught in Quaker schools and communities for many years and kept a poustinia, a retreat house for travelers, at their lakeside home in Wisconsin. Ken is a member of Stillwater Meeting, Ohio Yearly Meeting, currently sojourning with Beloit Meeting, Northern Yearly Meeting.

Allison Randall

Allison Randall is a member of Keene Friends Meeting in Keene, New Hampshire, a longtime member of New England Yearly Meeting Ministry and Counsel, and a leader of workshops on deepening meetings for worship and the spiritual lives of Quakers and non-Quakers. She also designs and makes soothing cloth centering toys and holds individuals and groups in the Light.

Appendix E: Finding a Quaker Charism at the Wild Goose Festival

While attending a festival that was a meeting place for people of faith who are committed to social justice and who also appreciate the expressive arts, Viv Hawkins became more aware of the value of the mutual spiritual accountability groups she had encountered and taught in a Quaker context. In this piece, she explains why this small group practice can help us face the challenges of the future.

This is an abridged version of Viv Hawkins's article published in *Friends Journal* December 1, 2013, https://www.friendsjournal.org/finding-quaker-charism-wild-goose-festival/.

Finding a Quaker Charism at the Wild Goose Festival

by Viv Hawkins

Certain characteristics of Friends practices began to fit effortlessly together for me in 2011 at the first Wild Goose Festival held in Shakori Hills, North Carolina. There, "at the intersection of justice, spirituality, art, and music," where people, most of whom identified as Christian, gathered to experience the Holy Spirit, I saw the gift that a particular practice . . . may be to the wider world.

Phyllis Tickle, an energetic religious professor and author, . . . heralded the coming time as one in which the human race will be radically changed. Referring to mainstream religion, she emphasized the leap involved in completing the Trinity by embracing Spirit. Pointing to the change which coincided with Jesus's life and the birth of Christianity and every 500-year period since, she spoke about the emerging church needing to powerfully reinvent itself. . . .

The following day, Leo Brunnick, founder and chief executive of Patheos, an online destination for global dialogue about religion and spirituality, spoke of the logarithmic rate of technological change. . . . Brunnick put this rate of change, with technology impacting medicine and other sciences, in the context of religion: "We need to ask, 'What more will we take out of God's hands?'"

It became apparent to me that our species will undergo heightened anxiety from this accelerating rate of change, and also from the economic and ecological challenges of rampant extinction and gross wealth disparities. Brunnick spoke about the way that groups tend to intensify and become exaggerated forms of themselves during times of rapid change; for example, fundamentalists can become more fundamentalistic, atheists more atheistic. In such demanding conditions, it may become more challenging to find that which unifies us as Quakers.

Moral questions will become more complex when the conversation shifts, for instance, from whether gays and lesbians can marry to whether clones and cyborgs can be clergy or senators. To reach across the resulting divides, a widespread and deep level of spiritual grounding will become imperative. . . As challenges become more complex and demanding, the collective intelligence of groups will be more critical to our planet's survival. Singular individuals in leadership roles may not suffice, as one person often does not have the needed breadth of wisdom or degree of trust which a group is better equipped to offer. But, perhaps, with new methods made possible by the open capacity of the Internet and cells of faithful groups who continually hold each other accountable to a higher good, the church can effectively unify, and humanity can become one and fully recognize its interdependence with all of creation.

At the time of the 2011 Wild Goose Festival, I was studying the effects of anxiety on individuals and systems in an attempt to countermand the related symptoms (or the condition itself). On a macro-level, I wanted to understand how larger groups can break through the apocalyptic tension felt in the world today. On a more personal level, I wanted to alleviate my own anxiety, the result of living without health insurance or other employee benefits on a gross salary of $216 per week among people with greater wealth. One saving grace during that difficult time for me was belonging to a network of communities of spiritual accountability which held its members to faithfulness even in our fear. This arrangement let us combine our small slices of truth into a larger portion and allowed us to share spiritual and material resources.

As I received the messages of Tickle and Brunnick, as I sang hymns and drank beer, as I danced with and assisted in his dementia one of the most brilliant people I knew, I was convinced that spiritual accountability, a practice I had come to know through Friends, needed to be spread like wildfire within our religious society. It also needed to be carried outward to help heal our wounded world. It provides a way to raise up good by holding those who serve and lead accountable to the highest possible outcome. To me, this practice of spiritual accountability seemed to embody a Quaker *charism*, an extraordinary power given by the Holy for the good of the world.

Friends believe in the inner goodness of every person and in the fuller knowledge and experience of our shared goodness when we intentionally seek, share, and act together on behalf of a greater good. We recognize that gifts conferred upon a community are to be nurtured by the community in service to the world. We acknowledge that leadership can arise through any one of us. The combination of these beliefs leads us to practice the power of the collective. These are the building blocks of collective intelligence. Might such a group process, which uses these practices in service to the Holy, be a Quaker charism?

Friend Parker Palmer, an author, educator, and activist, has shared the Quaker clearness process with the world through his writings and workshops. Many are well served by his work. Yet, clearness is just a first step in a leading. It is possible to hear a sacred call and be found clear to proceed and yet still forsake it because of the noise of our fears. We might abandon it for the promise of power, privilege, or the consumer culture that encircles us. A spiritual accountability process can offer a centripetal force to pull us back toward our sacred path.

An on-going spiritual accountability group which both supports and challenges us can be a much more powerful force for long-term faithfulness than a brief clearness committee. Because it is a concerted and continuous commitment, each individual can come to intimately know his or her own and other members' strengths and opportunities for growth. This level of commitment allows members to accompany one another in the field while offering ministry.

I call this kind of relationship "peer spiritual accountability," and it has offered me and others fuller portions of truth at times when it was most needed. In addition, the practice of spiritual accountability has at times abated my anxiety and, at other times, actually acted as an antidote to the formation of anxiety. It surely was an important resource that furthered the ministry carried by the six members of a peer group which met monthly for about seven years.

We were a self-appointed group serving in various ministries. A structured and agreed-upon spiritual accountability process helped us midwife each other's on-going calls and venture outside our comfort zones. Our main queries were: "What does faithfulness ask of Spirit?" and "How will we respond?" We took turns, rotating our focus on two members for each two-hour monthly session. These sessions opened with a period of worship and closed with a self-assessment of our attention to our guiding principles. Deep listening and attention to the presenter's words, body language, changes in skin tone such as blushing or flushing, and the movement of the Spirit in the gathered group all guided our waiting worship. The attention prompted questions and occasional observations from those of us who were present to the presenter.

Our overall intent was to help the focus person find the way to the feet of the Inward Teacher, to confront the Source of Being, to directly encounter the Guide. As such, questions or observations were pointed in that direction rather than toward answering questions we might have or toward solving problems. Being inextricably committed, irrevocably vulnerable, and consummately loving were prerequisites for the experience offering its fullest gifts. In those sacred encounters, some of us took notes for the presenter and other group members to reference afterward. Like a set of flip cards that create a movie when displayed in sequence, these notes showed the growth in the Spirit, as well as the places where we had yet to venture—individually and as a group.

Other groups appointed by our monthly meetings provide a different kind of accountability structure. As a member of Central Philadelphia (Pa.) Meeting, I've participated in a "spiritual accountability group" (SAG), with its primary functions being to assist in accountability:

- between the ministry and the One who calls us to ministry

- between the ministry and those served by it

- between the minister and the faith community

I have tried to incorporate coaching components into this SAG process, so that we will hold one another accountable not only to Spirit but also to project progress (both the outcomes and the manner in which those outcomes are achieved).

Some of us have also engaged in shorter term groups of peer accountability. One group used check-in telephone calls every few weeks; another worked as a team to create a six-month program on Spirit-led social action. Together, these interlocking groups formed a safety net; members knew they were being held both by Spirit and by a community of friends. These groups served us and others in unimaginable and often indescribable ways. They midwifed plays, workshops, courses, plenary talks, articles and books, and service in urban schools, prisons, conference centers, on committees and boards, and amid families in need. They helped us, with Divine assistance, to co-create a better world.

The world yearns for greater connection. I often hear Friends expressing a need for spiritual accountability on the local meeting level. . . . [In interest groups on releasing ministry at Quaker gatherings,] [w]e heard many participants speak of the need for love, respect, trust, vulnerability, honesty, witnessing others on the path, and a sense of safety. All of these relationship characteristics deepen and become more nuanced and intimate over time as we continuously devote ourselves to each other's faithfulness. They become reciprocal when we use a peer process for mutual spiritual accountability.

What is needed for greater spiritual accountability within and beyond the Religious Society of Friends? More of what has already begun. Trainings on peer spiritual accountability have been offered to groups in many different faith communities. . . .

In a world starved for community and seeking alternatives to the dominant culture, we're asked by the Spirit to spread the good news. The spiritual accountability process and the cells of community that are formed by it create a "plausibility structure" that opens people to another way of being: one that supports the individual and the collective yearning for the Divine and encourages us to shift from an economy of mammon—marked by a scarcity mentality and material greed—to an economy of manna—marked by an abundance mentality and the formation of beneficial relationships and community.

Spiritual accountability groups invite us to break down the false boundaries that separate us. They offer the opportunity to create alternative communities that challenge the dominant paradigm. They offer the opportunity to seek not only our highest personal selves, but also *sarvodaya*, which in Hindi means "the good of all." Faced with the challenges of our time, we need to evolve individually and as a species as effectively and rapidly as we can. The peer spiritual accountability model offers the antidote to separateness and reaches toward true community, the Sacred Oneness, the Sh'ma that says, "The Lord our God is one God," and helps us know: "It is GOOD!"

I agree with Tickle and Brunnick that the changes our world is experiencing will increase in complexity and frequency in the future and require us to be more resilient individuals, groups, and societies. I believe that these peer spiritual accountability groups offer a unique democratic promise as we live into a future full of change, fear, and risk of entrenchment and division. These groups assist the individuals within them to evolve in several ways: by allowing our fullest selves to be revealed, by learning from one another, and by sharing resources that otherwise might seem scarce.

Spiritual accountability prepares us in ways we have not previously known, guided by the Guide and our shared wisdom, to leverage our diversity for the highest good.

Appendix F: Restoring the Ecology of Faithfulness

Quakerism began in seventeenth-century England and soon spread to other parts of the world, sustained not only by gifted individuals willing to take risks but also by a radically faithful community. Benjamin Warnke here describes several practices, including faithfulness groups, that contribute to an ecosystem of faithfulness. In his view, the most important element is love.

This piece has not been previously published.

Restoring the Ecology of Faithfulness

by Benjamin Warnke

My dear brethren and sisters, to whom my love abounds, I am filled with pure love unto you all, dear lambs; feel it in your own lives, and receive it into your own hearts as new oil; for truly the fear of the Lord is our strength, and the blessing of the Lord is our portion, which the Lord doth daily give unto us, blessed be His name forever. Oh, let us all keep in lowliness, and meekness, and tender love, one towards another, which is the seal and witness that the Lord is with us, where the Lord forever keeps us staid upon Him, to receive our daily bread, which satisfieth the hungry soul. Dear friends, brethren, and sisters, this I am constrained to let you know, how mightily the love of the Lord our God abounds in my heart, and from my life towards you all; it runs forth as a living stream, refreshing the Spirit and life of us all, and every one as you feel it, and according to your measures, receive it into your hearts, to the refreshing and strengthening of one another.

—William Robinson, Boston, 1659

Quakers are told ours was a radical faith; certainly the lives of early Quakers George Fox, James Nayler, Margaret Fell, Mary Dyer, and William Robinson would suggest as much. At its beginning, Quakerism was radical—and it may still be—in the belief that God is available to us, unmediated, as whole and present for us as the Spirit was for the prophets; radical in its expression, in the directness and equality of the language of early Friends; radical in the conviction that anyone—a woman, a child— could respond to and articulate the divine; and radical also, in a way that we may have lost some sense of today, in the kind of community that Quaker testimonies imagined and encouraged. Among the testimonies that Quakers esteem and espouse— simplicity, integrity, equality, to name a few—it is strange that we no longer speak of love. Early Friends did. The strength and joy that they sought and found in one another, in community, may be what we require if we are to recover some of the life and vibrancy—and radical sense of purpose—of early Friends.

The desert fathers discovered the divine in the wastelands, far from the distractions of civilization, insulated from the joys and frustrations of human interaction. The benefits of this retreat seem not without costs: isolation, if not intentional and limited, surely entails some diminishment of the physical and emotional, some loss of what it means to be fully human. While I imagine one can meet the Spirit in solitude, I am not sure how one lives with it there. Wherever we encounter the divine, we nurture, share, and celebrate it in community. We make love visible in our lives with each other.

I read some time ago of an experiment that recreated an oak savanna, once a common but now quite rare ecosystem in the Midwest; when the basic elements of this environment were restored—oak, hickory, and persimmon trees and native grasses and wildflowers—an entire world of vanished plants, birds, insects, and animals returned, as if by spontaneous generation. Perhaps Friends can create a restored ecosystem of the Spirit that would spark a comparable rebirth.

I'm persuaded that this renewal would begin with love; that we are for each other vital and necessary companions in our mutual search for the divine; that we have to animate and strengthen our connections with each other. We need to become vulnerable, to find courage, to allow our gifts to flourish, to know that we require one another. If we can live together like this, perhaps the Spirit will blossom among us. While Quaker precepts might be promulgated to allow for a clearer and more immediate relationship with God, perhaps they are first if not foremost integral to our relationships with each other.

It seems clear that any attempt to create a blessed community—the peaceable kingdom—begins with love; it seems predictable also that we would fail again and again in our efforts to realize this ideal. Yet isn't this what we are called to do, as a faith community, as Quakers—to try once more to see what love can achieve?

How can a community nurture the worship, faith, and faithfulness of its members and attenders? How can it contribute intentionally to the life of the Spirit?

Over the past year and a half, a disparate group of Quakers from different meetings, guided by some experienced Friends, has experimented with several practices familiar to early Quakers as part of an effort to expand our ability to answer these questions. These practices have included

Extended Worship: We have gathered in worship for two hours or occasionally longer. I have been surprised to find the first hour of a two-hour meeting for worship the longest. During the span of the meeting, I have felt an increasing sense of groundedness and have been filled with a sense of connection that has grown into a feeling of caring and nurture for the meeting as a whole and for its individual members;

Vocal Intercessory Prayer: We have explored saying prayers aloud for each other in a close, connected circle. While most of us have found this a powerful, binding experience, many also have discovered that vocal prayer is an unfamiliar, sometimes awkward experience. Asking the divine to intercede actively on behalf of one of us has felt alien to Quaker practice as we have known it. Despite these impediments, we have been able to acknowledge the power of our collective prayer and to grow over time in our ability to pray aloud;

Elders/Ministers: The example of our teachers and elders has been revelatory. Their commitment to lives of the Spirit, to ministry, to their callings, has opened up possibilities for our own faith and leadings that had hitherto been concealed or faintly discerned;

Faithfulness Groups: We have formed faithfulness groups, four or five of us in each. Over time, I have been deeply moved by the intimacy and trust that has grown in these fellowships. I have come to know well several members of the meeting whom I knew only slightly and to spend rich and emotional time with them. Beyond the direct and significant rewards of the faithfulness group itself, the connections sparked by my involvement have deepened my relationships with other Friends in my meeting.

Love is reciprocal. It is like cloud-to-ground lightning: it originates in two places at once. I have felt, even as my own faith has grown, an encouragement from my spiritual community to share my leadings, as well as an invitation to participate more fully and deeply in the life of the whole. The willingness of my fellow faithfulness group participants to share aspects of their spiritual journeys has inspired me. The faith that they have shared and shown has encouraged me to seek and name my own faith. Their ability and readiness to acknowledge and share their spiritual gifts have allowed me to acknowledge and share my own.

Our journeys are often lonely, confused and hard. We live too often apart from one another, struggling in solitude to make sense of an experience that we apprehend as solitary but is not. Only our connections to each other help to steady and guide us. Only in our ability to see God in each other are we able to discern God in ourselves; only in acknowledging that of God in ourselves are we able to find the divine elsewhere and everywhere. Early Friends seem to have experienced this connectedness, to have fashioned an interconnected ecosystem where the Spirit flourished. Surely we can do this again.

Benjamin Warnke

Benjamin Warnke is a member of Brooklyn Friends Meeting (New York). He is a trustee of the Mary McDowell Friends School, a board member of the American Friends Service Committee, and a member of the Haverford College Corporation. He formerly served as chair of the board of Brooklyn Friends School.

Acknowledgments

I give big thanks to Viv Hawkins, Benjamin Warnke, Ken Jacobsen, Allison Randall, Emma Churchman, and Margery Post Abbott for permission to include their writings in this book.

I give thanks, also, for all I have learned from the Shalem Institute's Spiritual Guidance Program, especially the format for peer groups.

I give thanks to the Lyman Fund, which gave me a grant in 1996 that helped make it possible for me to participate in Shalem's Spiritual Guidance Program. Twenty-two years later, they gave me a second grant to support the writing of this book.

I give thanks to Newtown Square Friends Meeting, Chestnut Hill Friends Meeting, and now Swarthmore Friends Meeting for their support, each in turn, of my ministry of spiritual nurture. I give thanks to those Friends who have participated in the support and oversight committees appointed by those meetings and to all the individual Friends who have contributed in so many ways, material as well as spiritual, to make this work possible. I am grateful to the Anne Bernstein Richan Peace Action Fund for a grant to support my writing.

Many institutions have contributed to my ongoing learning about how to cultivate and support faithfulness. I especially want to thank Pendle Hill Retreat and Study Center for all I have learned there, as well as the School of the Spirit and the Friends General Conference Traveling Ministries program (now laid down). I am deeply grateful to Woolman Hill Retreat Center for hosting two nine-month programs I led on nurturing faithfulness.

I give thanks to Laura Melly, my partner in expanding the peer group model, in creating the Way of Ministry program, and in sharing peer groups among Friends. I'm grateful to others who joined that work, including Beckey Phipps, Ken and Katharine Jacobsen, and Barbarajene Williams. I appreciate and have learned from how Viv Hawkins and Lola Georg have expanded the model in their teachings on mutual spiritual accountability groups.

I give thanks to all those who have participated in peer groups and faithfulness groups with me, including Connie Lezenby, Renee Crauder, Esther Darlington, Janet Stokes, Laura Melly, Michael Wajda, Alison Levie, Michael Gibson, Barry Crossno, Joe Garren, Stacy Nagel, Anne Harper, Rebecca Mays, Beth Popelka, Viv Hawkins, Hollister Knowlton, Martha Lee Kemper, Carolyn Schodt, Diann Herzog, Paulette Meier, Rhonda Pfaltzgraff-Carlson, Eric Evans, and Angela York Crane. I give thanks to those who participated in the Way of Ministry and the Nurturing Worship, Faith, and Faithfulness programs and who have taken the faithfulness group practice out into the world in wonderful ways. I have learned so much from all of you about growing into faithfulness and becoming what God intends for us.

I am grateful to all who participated in my survey about faithfulness groups and whose quotes are included in this book. In addition to a number of the Friends named above, they include Tammy Forner, Paula Rossvall, Julie Heagney, and Benjamin Warnke.

I am thankful for the careful, helpful copyediting by Kathy McKay, who brought more clarity to this text.

I am deeply grateful to Charles Martin, editor of Inner Light Books, for making my writing available to a wider audience. I give thanks for his faithfulness when God led him to become a publisher of books about Quakerism.

I give thanks for the faithful, enduring love of my husband, Terry Hauger. His support of me and of the work involved was crucial in the creation of this book.

None of my work would have been possible without the life-long love and support of my parents, Jean and Charlie Martin.

Notes

1 Jonathan Merritt, "It's Getting Harder to Talk About God," *The New York Times*, Oct. 13, 2018, https://www.nytimes.com/2018/10/13 /opinion/sunday/talk-god-sprituality-christian.html.

2 This program is now called Nurturing the Call: Spiritual Guidance Program. More information is available on the Shalem Institute website at https://shalem.org/programs/longterm/nurturing-the-call-spiritual-guidance-program/.

3 The Way of Ministry program was held under the joint care of the School of the Spirit Ministry and Pendle Hill Retreat Center.

4 Douglas Van Steere, *Where Words Come From: An Interpretation of the Ground and Practice of Quaker Worship and Ministry*, Swarthmore Lecture (London: Allen and Unwin, 1955), 14.

5 For a good discussion of the types of questions that can help with discernment, including "evocative questions," see appendix 2 of Suzanne G. Farnham, Joseph P. Gill, R. Taylor McLean, and Susan M. Ward, *Listening Hearts: Discerning Call in Community* (New York: Morehouse Publishing, 1991).

6 Jeremy Taylor, *Where People Fly and Water Runs Uphill: Using Dreams to Tap the Wisdom of the Unconscious* (New York: Warner Books, 1992), 53–59.

7 The stories of the visions of Peter and Cornelius are told in Acts 10.

8 For more information, see the Baltimore Yearly Meeting Spiritual Formation Program website, https://www.bym-rsf.org/events /spiritform/ and the Philadelphia Yearly Meeting Spiritual Formation Program Collaborative website, https://www.pym.org/spiritual-formation-program-collaborative/.

9 For more information, see the Experiment with Light website, http://www.experiment-with-light.org.uk/resource.htm.

Also available from Inner Light Books

A Word from the Lost
By David Lewis
        ISBN 978-1-7328239-7-6 (hardcover)
        ISBN 978-1-7328239-8-3 (paperback)
        ISBN 978-1-7328239-9-0 (eBook)

William Penn's 'Holy Experiment'
by James Proud
        ISBN 978-0-9998332-9-2 (hardcover)
        ISBN 978-1-7328239-3-8 (paperback)

In the Stillness: Poems, prayers, reflections
by Elizabeth Mills
        ISBN 978-1-7328239-0-7 (hardcover)
        ISBN 978-1-7328239-1-4 (paperback)
        ISBN 978-1-7328239-2-1 (eBook)

Walk Humbly, Serve Boldly: Modern Quakers as Everyday Prophets
by Margery Post Abbott
        ISBN 978-0-9998332-6-1 (hardcover)
        ISBN 978-0-9998332-7-8 (paperback)
        ISBN 978-0-9998332-8-5 (eBook)

Primitive Quakerism Revived
by Paul Buckley
        ISBN 978-0-9998332-2-3 (hardcover)
        ISBN 978-0-9998332-3-0 (paperback)
        ISBN 978-0-9998332-5-4 (eBook)

Primitive Christianity Revived
by William Penn
Translated into Modern English by Paul Buckley
        ISBN 978-0-9998332-0-9 (hardcover)
        ISBN 978-0-9998332-1-6 (paperback)
        ISBN 978-0-9998332-4-7 (eBook)

Jesus, Christ and Servant of God
Meditations on the Gospel According to John
by David Johnson
        ISBN 978–0–9970604–6–1 (hardcover)
        ISBN 978–0–9970604–7–8 (paperback)
        ISBN 978–0–9970604–8–5 (eBook)

The Anti-War
by Douglas Gwyn
        ISBN 978-0-9970604-3-0 (hardcover)
        ISBN 978-0-9970604-4-7 (paperback)
        ISBN 978-0-9970604-5-4 (eBook)

Our Life Is Love, the Quaker Spiritual Journey
by Marcelle Martin
> ISBN 978-0-9970604-0-9 (hardcover)
> ISBN 978-0-9970604-1-6 (paperback)
> ISBN 978-0-9970604-2-3 (eBook)

A Quaker Prayer Life
by David Johnson
> ISBN 978-0-9834980-5-6 (hardcover)
> ISBN 978-0-9834980-6-3 (paperback)
> ISBN 978-0-9834980-7-0 (eBook))

The Essential Elias Hicks
by Paul Buckley
> ISBN 978-0-9834980-8-7 (hardcover)
> ISBN 978-0-9834980-9-4 (paperback)
> ISBN 978-0-9970604-9-2 (eBook)

The Journal of Elias Hicks
edited by Paul Buckley
> ISBN 978-0-9797110-4-6 (hardcover)
> ISBN 978-0-9797110-5-3 (paperback)

Dear Friend: The Letters and Essays of Elias Hicks
edited by Paul Buckley
> ISBN 978-0-9834980-0-1 (hardcover)
> ISBN 978-0-9834980-1-8 (paperback)

The Early Quakers and 'the Kingdom of God'
by Gerard Guiton
> ISBN 978-0-9834980-2-5 (hardcover)
> ISBN 978-0-9834980-3-2 (paperback)
> ISBN 978-0-9834980-4-9 (eBook)

John Woolman and the Affairs of Truth
edited by James Proud
> ISBN 978-0-9797110-6-0 (hardcover)
> ISBN 978-0-9797110-7-7 (paperback)

Cousin Ann's Stories for Children by Ann Preston
edited by Richard Beards
illustrated by Stevie French
> ISBN 978-0-9797110-8-4 (hardcover),
> ISBN 978-0-9797110-9-1 (paperback)

Counsel to the Christian-Traveller: also Meditations and Experiences
by William Shewen
> ISBN 978-0-9797110-0-8 (hardcover)
> ISBN 978-0-9797110-1-5 (paperback)

CPSIA information can be obtained
at www.ICGtesting.com
Printed in the USA
LVHW090557081019
633405LV00008B/3568/P